NICK SANDERS

Notes & Pictures

PARALLEL COAST

NICK SANDERS

Notes & Pictures

PARALLEL COAST

Acknowledgements

Books and accompanying films like Parallel Coast do not happen without real help from commercial benefactors. They help keep the price right and contribute to the 'arts' in the motorcycle world and for this I am really grateful. So thanks as ever to my own sponsors; Geoff Selvidge and Simon Belton at Yamaha, Simon Jackson, Rebecca Donahue and David Newman at Carole Nash Insurance, Neville Evans at Cambrian Tyres along with Andreas Faulstich at Continental Europe and Michael Walshaw at Hein Gericke. Thank you for your kind support. I also wish to thank David Morley at Renntec and Andre Waszczyszyn at Webbs Motorcycles.

Especial thanks to Paul Blezard for making such a good job of the edit and Elgan Griffiths for the design. Also thanks to Chippy Wood for the bike photos, Joshua Wyborn for the black and white photos and everyone at MRM Graphics for working so hard on this publication. Special secret thanks and love to Caroline.

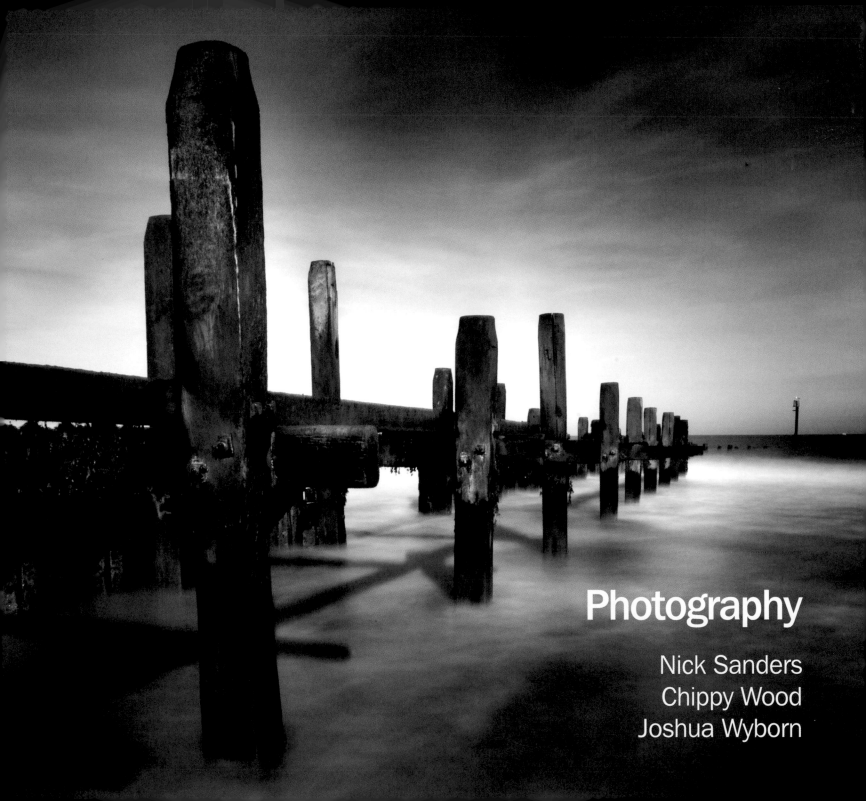

Photography

Nick Sanders
Chippy Wood
Joshua Wyborn

For Max & Miles

Introduction

As you might expect, this journey is not a conventional one. It never intended to follow every inch of the coast, just bits that took my fancy. Sometimes I missed out a small area because it was raining. I stayed overlong elsewhere because there were either lots of tea shops, loads of bikers to talk to or because I liked sitting on a bench beside my bike looking out to sea. I make no apology for the historical nature of the text. After I've ridden my nice new R1, had my tea and eaten my chips, I wanted to know more about the place where I live. My research tries to examine Englishness (I am less qualified to attempt Welshness and Scottishness) and I have tried to challenge the conventional way of describing a motorcycle journey. There is bound to be a quote about 'not being afraid to fail' and in the process of failing you occasionally might succeed ... I can handle that. Thanks and enjoy.

H

UNSTANTON IS A quiet Victorian resort and is the only town in East Anglia that faces west, across The Wash, towards Boston and Lincolnshire. Riding down the main street, you are greeted by chip shops and a tattoo parlour. Geographically misplaced, the 'Tamworth Tearooms' stand alongside the village green next to other small shops. With little or no plan other than some vague blueprint in my head about motorcycling around the coast of Britain, I start another journey.

It looks like a tidy town and you soon begin to suspect the excitement of living here is connected to that. In the way bikers like clean bikes, people like tidy places. It suggests 'safe, yet hardworking'. Clean streets are predictable streets, and the knowledge that they will be swept clean on some regular basis allows for a feeling of order. In places like Hunstanton, one week might be a tad less tidy than previously, prompting locals to *harrumph*. A letter would be sent to the editor of the local paper and the headline *'Litter Bin Kicked Over By Vandals'* would make that week's edition, along with conclusions about the curse of disaffected youths popping screaming wheelies on their mopeds.

Victorian England would have been equally hysterical. Successive generations bemoan the demise of the 'good old days'. Most people had neither the time nor the means to go away on holiday before the second half of the 19th century, but after the railway arrived here in 1862, this resort began to grow thanks to the temporary influx of people from King's Lynn and Norwich.

The local landowners were the Le Strange family who were largely responsible for the town's development. Not so long ago notices on the beach still proclaimed the family's rights to all the mussels and oysters on the foreshore, and anything that was thrown up onto the beach during a storm was also theirs to keep. As hereditary Lord High Admirals of The Wash, the Le Stranges could also claim possession over anything in the sea as far as a man could ride his horse at low tide, and then throw his spear. There are lots of perks in Hunstanton, if you're a Le Strange.

Much has been written about the 2009 version of Yamaha's R1. It has the new and MotoGP-derived cross-plane crankshaft, complete with sophisticated fuelling and smart electronic control which are instantly evident when you twist the throttle. Around the lanes on the coast of Norfolk between villages coated with the poshness of a Chelsea-by-the-Sea, the bike feels faster and gruntier than the one on which I went around the world last year.

It was hard to truly road test such a bike on the lanes that separate Britain from the sea. Every narrow bend risks a car coming the opposite way. This isn't a long story about riding a bike fast, it's a short tale about riding a fast bike slowly.

Out of town, the cliffs at Lighthouse Lane are layer-caked with red chalk sandwiched between its white equivalent and a type of brown sandstone called carr stone. On the tops, the remains of St Edmund's Chapel, built after Edmund landed here in AD 850, lie next to the white lighthouse. In the old part of town, red-roofed fishing cottages stand next to the church with Hunstanton Hall dating back to Tudor times. Suddenly, almost too soon into the journey, I have an overwhelming feeling that the coast of Britain is a 'land which time forgot'. Some motorcycle adventures are like secret treasures, during the unearthing of which, there is much sifting of dust.

Some motorcycle adventures are like secret treasures, during the unearthing of which, there is much sifting of dust.

DOWN THE ROAD at Wells-next-the-Sea the occasional car rumbles down a narrow street and disappears out of sight. It is a pretty summer evening with a chill wind but this light has the luminescence of innocence. It is easy to take photographs of colourful things; a red telephone box against a blue sky, the juxtaposition of green hawthorn and brown, a shop painted yellow and blue. This reminds me of an important objective of such a gentle voyage, which is to be re-acquainted with the concept of Englishness whilst in England and whether this can be judged by the only two attributes I might know anything about: character and landscape. Scottishness and Welshness will have a different flavour, but the significant third ingredient in this layered coastal cake is the bike.

The grunt of the engine rips wildly across manicured little villages like a bad boy on the pull.

Perhaps amplified by the quietness of this laid-back part of the country, the grunt of the engine rips wildly across manicured little villages like a bad boy on the pull. On the long bumpy straights, the sound has 'naughty' written all over its face, cascading loudly when it takes a corner. This bike doesn't talk, it shouts. The cross-plane crank takes away the flywheel effect of the flattening top dead centre and although there is less torque, the immediate pick-up on revs counteracts a feeling I'd intuitively known for years.

Landscape is the easier of the two other attributes. A view is the totality of visible objects – roads, trees, fields, houses, lakes and churches – not just the land. Throughout history it has been supposed that landscapes shape human perception, that the power of the earth was greater than the heavens in determining human destiny.

As I sit by my bike beside salt marshes listening to the wind tease flying wires on the mainsails of small yachts, I feel the need to be a traveller sneaking up on me.

Close by, Burnham Market has the mannerisms of a Chelsea-on-Sea. It is a place mesmerised by such a sense of self-worth, it gives off a feeling of separateness. Nearby, The Lord Nelson pub serves beer through a hatch as if it were grog on board HMS Victory. Before Nelson went to battle, he was a Norfolk lad. He was born here, the sixth of eleven children, and he was educated until the age of twelve at nearby North Walsham, thirty miles to the east. That night I am to be the guest of Mrs Plum. She owns the original site of the rectory in which Nelson was born. Nina Plum is a plum farmer and every one of her plums is hand-picked; when she harvests, she takes baskets of plums to market. Certain plums are picked ahead of others, and knowing that the ripening process of different types of plums are not always the same, picking can be staggered, so in between her plum-picking, she can plan how and when she will ride her motorcycle. Mrs Plum, along with her friend Clive, once motorcycled around the world. They recently returned from their adventures in the Americas, and when the plums are picked, will think nothing of doing it again.

The venerable Bede was born in Northumbria in 672 and his Historia Ecclesiastica Gentis Anglorum or 'Ecclesiastical History of the English People' is generally thought to be the earliest written account of the English; although written in Latin, Bede also translated many works into his native Anglo-Saxon. More recently, four runes scratched on the back of a brooch dating from 650 and found in an Anglo-Saxon burial ground are now thought to be the earliest example of written English. The story of Beowulf, a poem dating from around 700 is the oldest and best known piece of Old English literature. Historians have said that the English movement was for decoration rather than architecture – analogous to how nice looking English bikes used to sit in a pool of oil in the shadow of Japanese-ness. This is form over function and unlike engineering, eloquent prose is more concerned with making patterns from fragments of knowledge without needing to make perfect sense. This is how I see journeys; elegant and sometimes mysterious.

It is the ice-cream-obviousness of what's easy to see that I don't get. Motorcycling around the coast of Britain could easily be described in the context of a *'Kiss-Me-Quick'* culture, of red telephone boxes and chip shops, shingle beaches by the seashore and cafés. There are bikers by the dozen and mums pushing children in their prams. I hear seagulls bark over the din of crashing waves yet acknowledgement of a journey has to be more than the sum total of stereotype. Historical authors such as Ackroyd are experts when speaking of the English imagination. They talk about purity of function undermined by elaboration of form – all fur and no knickers.

These people talk about something which avoids *'depth of feeling or profundity of argument in favour of artifice and rhetorical display'*. It is the irregular beauty I seek or a moment in a place unvisited by others. For me this is about a Parallel Coast, two ways of thinking about the same thing.

Bike built in Japan. Journey made in Britain.

THE R1 HAS a mode-mapping switch which acts like three different throttle cams on the twist grip. This effectively means you can select a different power delivery for a given amount of throttle. 'B' mode provides a lazy slow gathering of speed whilst standard for me is below par for a bike of this class. 'A' mode pushes your eyes to the back of your head while your testicles disappear to God knows where. As you approach the speed of light, the colour spectrum alters, the bike starts to shorten and there is true fear in your stomach as you meet yourself on the way back from a place you haven't yet reached. As I slow down with a 'squishshsh' from the brakes, I notice over the hedgerows how flat fields lead to a very big sky.

North of the Broads is a landscape of flatness and my view of the day. Cattle graze on meadows reclaimed from the sea, and protected by a defensive barrier of sand and shingle, marsh grasses lead to the road across from which lush meadows appear to move like the arms of a Mexican Wave. Beyond the wall, sand spits are toyed-with by high tides, re-forming the coastline twice every 24 hours leaving behind salt flats that form estates of waders, avocets and marsh harriers. For the most part it is a land of flatness and big skies. It is a space bounded by fences and gate posts that look as if they've been there for hundreds of years.

Turning left and downhill into Wells, the street narrows. People, clearly familiar with each other, suggest a general air of ease. When the sun pops out from behind a cloud, it burnishes out the grey to highlight carefully painted primary hues. Traders' signs are an array of vermillion and emerald, some in yellows and purple but all highlight the 'bucket and spade' approach to colour close to the seaside. At the bottom of this cobbled street, the amusement centre and rock-sellers line the small main road adjacent to the town harbour. Alongside fish and chip shops and cheap cafés, 'pay and display' car parks have become a quintessential feature of a functioning seaside town. In a shed behind the town I meet John Aldiss and his colleague. They are preparing to take a speedboat around the coast of Britain in 24 hours. That's faster than an R1.

These English villages have barely changed since I last rode around the coast in 2004. Such is the brittleness of modernity it's like marching into the future backwards hoping everything doesn't change; an Englishness for which newness is a mutation for the worse.

As with bikes, clothing and where you might go on holiday, the contrast between 'quaint' and 'cheap' is not only a demarcation of taste, but is like a schism which divides the idea of what a town is. Seaside places can be serious or silly, primitive in outlook yet robustly cosmopolitan, happy and sad, foolish yet somehow wise.

THE NORFOLK COAST is a sanctuary for small lanes that shoot off towards the sea. Every few minutes, yet another track, like a capillary, tempts you to follow. A short way from Wells, I ride into Morston Quay, a National Trust property. There is a bylaw that insists you sit here on benches with binoculars and a packed lunch, after which you follow on with a puff on a bent pot pipe. With the benign expression of church-goers, small groups of badge-wearers relax beatifically, as voluminous skies threaten to envelope us all.

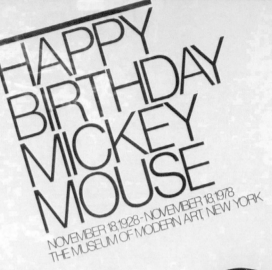

By Blakeley I am riding gently. I crossed the Nubian Desert in a different way but in truth, there was considerably less to look at. The way this bike expresses itself through the gears to a quick speed is the way you might use a sharp knife. The scalpel-like precision, with its throaty sound, is, if you get to know this bike really well, like dressing a wolf in lamb's clothing and for once I have time to listen. Pegging down a gear while shifting the mapping to the 'quick' setting is what this bike is all about. Whoever made this bike fathered a genius.

At Morston Quay, a large round chap comes close and asks, quite obliquely, if I know what I am doing. "Only sometimes," I say, not sure where this conversation is leading.

"Because I used to ride bikes you know, had all sorts. Once had a Sunbeam and although it took a while to get her warmed up, by jingo, when she was hot she really got going."
"Oh," I say.
"Yes, she would have any other bike licked, that's for sure."
"Licked?"
"Clean as a whistle, once she got going there was no stopping her."

This chap is elderly and has a ring of hair around the back of his head. He looked eccentric enough to be either deeply inbred, very clever or both and admits to being especially fascinated by lug worms. A doctor of zoology, he has spent all his childhood in this cove. He refuses to be photographed – "I have my detractors" – and mumbles something about an unforgivably unmentionably dreadful twin sister. On his 78th birthday and as a special treat, he punched her and blacked her eye, "Oh yes I did," and chuckles, "funny goings on in these parts", then says more darkly, "you should read the book *The Troublesome Priest* by Jonathan Tucker; my father gave him such a kicking that it led to him being de-frocked."

The inlet glistened in the sun and small boats motored out towards the sea. Here sailors skim along the edge of salt marsh, then in the distance their masts disappear behind bull-rushes and tall reeds. The scene was so English; the simple charm of small things. There are no world records for landscape in the English countryside because everything is considered and small; the small cottage, the tidy hedgerow and a little light afternoon tea. Everything is provided in small measures; the narrow brook, the little lanes bisecting small fields and the sense is that nothing is large enough to be grand.

The Flint Art Gallery in the small main street of Blakeley is run by a man with a double-barrelled name. It's a Home Counties operation in the wilds of East Anglia, and the exhibited works depict beach huts looking out to an ocean that is perfectly partnered with the land. I think the watercolours are especially expressive of the spirit of Englishness, their observations taken from small details: an oar, a rock, a feeling. It takes someone with time on their hands to present a different view, as the artist offers wide expanses of field and sky, which invite you to sense a different kind of space. In the distance, where they meet the sea, broad swathes of rough grass and reed form the only horizon, yet it is where the sea meets the sky that such margins of space become difficult to separate.

A little further south, the painter Gainsborough enjoyed Suffolk with its coloured air but it was Turner who influenced the landscape writing of Thomas Hardy in the West Country. He called Turner's works 'light modified by objects'. His feelings for Egdon Heath were putrified by the swamp, a haunting English vision that offered the opposite of hope. There, unlike here, is a more vengeful sky sweeping down from the moors. I wonder what Turner would have made of Hardy's heroine Eustacia Vye? But understanding what it is to be a settler here has to have some historical context. In Northumbria, around 700, the Venerable Bede wrote about a scarcely populated and poorly cultivated wasteland. The England of the Angles and Saxons was one of cold isolation of a large land inhabited by few.

Here in Norfolk, light close to the sea under big skies is of the highest quality, it sends out signals of brightness and possibility. Yet sitting under the menace of a storm building, the light tires in the afternoon, concurring with some melancholic sense of temporality and warm air. It is also a light that preens itself, like the paintings, taking on the texture of a canvas of dark cloud, and in such a way, the beauty of Norfolk has been exhaled for a thousand years.

Around here the roads do not have a lot of traffic. Sometimes you can open the throttle and take a corner by the scruff of its neck. By holding onto the handlebars and committing yourself to the apex, this bike will keep you on your seat until it is safe to straighten up. The man at the art gallery suggests I take afternoon tea up the road so I ride to Wiveton Hall Fruit Farm where, in a wooden café, nice girls serve salami with goats' cheese on a chilli jam sandwich with brown or white bread. There is also basil and chive pancakes filled with spinach and ricotta beautifully baked in cream and Parmesan sauce. Or, instead, how about a gougère pastry filled with asparagus, crème fraîche along with chives served with salad? Sometimes, anything's better than chips!

I park my bike by the window. It is such a magnificent machine made more so against this backdrop of frippery. Yes, it is all very nice, this little trip around the coast of Britain. It is a Kingdom of Quaint Things just here, but I wonder when it will turn into a Kingdom of Rust?

Along the A149 I chase the small steam loco from Weybourne to Sheringham, which is the eastern terminus and headquarters of the North Norfolk Railway Company. It is an easy race, bike and train, since the narrow roads are mired in traffic. At the station, crowds of people disembark from carriages which charmingly reflect a warm sun against its rippling coachwork. Old leather suitcases and trunks with buckled straps have been strategically placed to give the impression that we are in another time. Ancient adverts for long-gone cigarette brands suggest that this is not of now. Bang alongside a road that leads to a set of traffic lights and a pedestrian precinct is a wonderfully discordant reality. Isn't this what we do when we ride our bikes? Are we foolish enough to think that when we cock a leg over our metal horse we are the same person as when we are asked to do our domestic duties? The word 'motorcycle' is a rallying-cry for the dreaminess that compels us to ride.

At the station, crowds of people disembark from carriages which charmingly reflect a warm sun against its rippling coachwork.

Dreams drift in and out of the English imagination and in context it is what makes someone ride a motorcycle. In the final poem of Lewis Carroll's 'Through the Looking Glass' he writes;

Ever drifting down the stream –
Lingering in the golden gleam –
Life, what is it but a dream?

We are people in a dream, a nation of riders, people on a beach, ghostly figures that mingle in the mists of time.

Dream language can contain subversive themes in a superficially innocent content. This is English understatement. This is literally 'under the statement'.

Assaults of the established order or advertisements of sexual proclivities can be subtly described without the writer being discovered or 'outed'.

1) I'm a biker, but your secret is safe with me.
2) Remember the days when pubs hung notices on their doors that read 'No Bikers', well they still do, although sometimes it reads a bit posher, 'sorry, no motorcyclists.'

The poet Coleridge said, "I should much wish ... to float about along an infinite ocean ... & wake once in a million years for a few minutes – just to know I was going to sleep a million years more". In her bedlam vision, the author of Frankenstein, Mary Shelley, wrote "my imagination, unbidden, possessed and guided me, towards the 'hideous phantasm of a man'".

A letter from a French cleric written in 1178 and sent to Nicholas of St Albans gives an inkling of how the English attitude is linked to the sea:

'Your island is surrounded by water, and not unnaturally its inhabitants are affected by the nature of the element in which they live. Unsubstantial fantasies slide easily into their minds. They think their dreams to be visions, and their visions to be divine. We cannot blame them, for such is the nature of their land.'

For centuries the English were perceived as 'seers of visions'. The druidic priests were renowned for their visionary powers. The earliest histories were propped up by a vision. The goddess Diana appeared before Brutus to say that: 'Beyond the realm of Gaul, a land there lies, sea-girt it lies, where giants dwelt of old.' Crucially important figures in contemporary literature would discuss in a sober manner about angels and the like, willing no suspension of disbelief.

N SHERINGHAM, the youth hostel is full, so not having my tent I ride the few remaining miles to Cromer. I begin to sense that the part of the coast which is preciously wrapped in a twin-set and pearls, is nearly passed. The part of Britain baked in a cornucopia of chive pancakes and dressed crab, will soon be replaced by greasy breakfasts and mugs of tea. Lovely. I find a hotel in West Runton.

That English book of books, Bunyan's 'Pilgrim's Progress' is an encyclopaedia of dreams – 'and as I slept, I dreamed a dream' and I too sleep and dream.

The next day I ride to North Walsham to meet Steve Harmer who, along with his dad George, owns and runs the Norfolk Motorcycle Museum. His exhibits are housed in what looks like a large old shed, but it could be a Tardis. There are a lot of rusty bits attached to bikes crammed together on shelves; bike after bike after old bike. To others it is a treasure trove of wonderfulness that has taken him and his dad a lifetime to acquire. By his own

admission it is the scruffiest museum in the world, but what magic! AJS bits litter the way to where Steve makes the tea and oily things lie on top of the telephone.

This is one of the coolest museums that I've ever been to. If you want a piss you have to step over a crankcase and the toilet apparatus could have been a prop for *Slumdog Millionaire*. Instinctively I love the place and see the sparkle in the eye of a man who enjoys going into work every day. The spare parts department is not catalogued precisely, but as Steve says, everything is within approximately two feet of where it should be.

Instinctively I know that the world the English live in is definitely not made in Britain. Seaside towns, with their pedestrianised walkways and self-conscious, pseudo-antiquarian bric-a-brac, easily partner American-style burger bars. Wells is not like this but it starts in Cromer and continues in its vulgarity along the sea front of Great Yarmouth. As Jeremy Paxman says, 'a nation of shopkeepers has become a nation of checkout operators'. This is about service industry operatives unable to run up a suit, advise on clock repairs or anything useful other than something you buy and then throw away.

In my endeavour to stay on the road nearest to the coast I avoid all the signs directing me to major routes and end up in Yarmouth docks. By road, the 'coast of Britain' is actually a lot less tangible as a route than Land's End to John O'Groats or the A5. For much of the ride you see fields, hedgerows, trees, towns, villages and sometimes people behaving strangely in a rather burlesque way, but not the sea.

Beside the brick-built bonded warehouses I turn round, exiting past the Great Yarmouth Port Authority building on the right before turning left by the impressive Star Hotel. Across the way from the Two Bears pub, there is a bridge which crosses the river to the railway station where signs for Southtown direct you onto the A47. Taking the first fork left that looks as if it should find the sea, I am on the ubiquitously named Marine Parade amongst bungalows all called 'Seaview'. In fact they should be called 'Hedgeview' because that is what separates them from the tennis courts and the promenade. At Yallop Avenue I lose interest and leave.

The road south from Great Yarmouth to Lowestoft doesn't hug the beach as any good coast road should. Instead, it rips quickly through small industries and Tesco supermarkets to remind me of the parallel nature of Blake's green and pleasant land.

On the side of the road next to lorries kicking out fumes, advertising hoardings show lovely husbands and beautiful wives running through surf with their perfect children. I often wonder what you need to do to join that particular club and make a mental note to rob a bank and buy myself some better looking body parts.

When you travel around the world quickly there is a kind of classroom thinking, which says you cannot record what you see. Actually you can. Robert Dunlop once said to me that at 180 mph he could make out individual faces in the crowd. People like him live in a world that passes very fast. Landscape becomes a blur, which the mind learns to fashion into something it can understand. Interesting how two people see the same thing but interpret what they see in different ways. Riding around the world gave me insight into how my being there changed *being there*.

The bike is handling well. There is nothing it fears other than being ridden badly. The wind feeds enthusiastically through my helmet and every bump on the road translates up the chassis to my arms as a firm strong mechanical process, and it is this feedback which gives me a sense of control. Every second of riding is based on ever smaller particles of thought which contribute to an increasing awareness of being free. It's so relaxing being on such a capable machine that it gives you space in your head to think. Biking from Norfolk to Suffolk to Essex to Kent, some see Elgar, John Bull, Kipling, codes of conduct, Eton, whit-week walks, snobbery and net curtain twitching as one form of Englishness. Others think of fish and chips, a bottle of plonk, Reliant Robins, Beefeater Pubs and binge-drinking at the weekend as the English epitome. When D.H. Lawrence returned to his home town of Nottingham it prompted him to write: *'the real tragedy of England, as I see it, is the tragedy of ugliness ... ugly ideals, ugly hope, ugly love, ugly clothes, ugly furniture, ugly houses. The English character has failed to develop the real urban side of a man ... yet they don't know how to build a city, how to think of one, or how to live in one. They are all suburban, pseudo-cottagey, and not one of them knows how to be truly urban'.* Knowing how Lawrence felt made me think of all the places on the coast where I just knew this would prove to be true.

Yet, in biker terms, we have the chance to migrate across this divide, cancel out the chaos of urban blight and crossover to the culture of the country. This Englishness might manifest itself on a Sunbeam or a Seeley or a ride to the café on a sunny Sunday and a quick expression of individuality out of sight of the old Bill.

Just before the town centre of Lowestoft, I turn left down what looks like a private road. At the bottom of the hill a street bears right onto Whapload Road, and here, tall town houses with elaborate balconies overlook a sea crisped by the light from an occasional sun. Winding back into the town and skirting around the fish docks I park in a café adjacent to the long promenade.

The first revelation of this little journey is that this is a land which time forgot, the second is the density of the subject. Wherever the coastal road separates itself from being in sight of the sea, it digresses every few miles like a seagull for fresh pickings. There is no end to the richness of the catch. On the narrow A12 towards Ipswich I turn down Angel Lane to Dunwich. It is narrow and a canopy of branches either side touch above to form a cathedral arch of trees. Signs warn of deer emerging from the forest while a fox trots ahead across the road.

The sound of the bike ricochets as if in a steep-sided valley and the echo filters into the thicket. On the right, a single row of houses signals the onset of the hamlet sandwiched by the museum and The Ship public house at the other end. Dead ends are not part of this agenda, but as long as there is a loop back out from the beach I will follow it.

There is a museum on the right as you pull into the village and further down the tiny main street, the road is directed to the beach. There, the wooden café is closing for the day so I park and stand by the ragged small cliffs and look out to sea.

Biking around the coast, or any journey for that matter, can have a sum that's greater than its parts. Ideally, bike plus rider plus journey should be made to equal something more than what has been accomplished in the past.

"Let
them
eat
cakes,"
someone shouted,
"bollocks
to that,"
they replied,
"give
us
ice
cream".

There is a cycle of events observable in any expedition. Here, when the Celts landed on these shores before the advent of historical dramas on BBC television, these chaps were viciously vexed with the Saxons for cutting down the forests to create the farmlands of East Anglia. And it was the Fenland farmers in turn who complained at the loss of fish due to the draining of the marshes. In a similar vein, 18th century peasants, forced to stand by as the 'Improvers' enforced the 'enclosures' so stealing their common land, they too were compromised, segregated as they were from traditional open pasture with a planting of the hawthorn hedgerow on such a scale as to be almost unimaginable for these peat-diggers of Norfolk.

A little north of here, pleasure craft motor around the Norfolk Broads. How many mariners know, that as holes in the ground, the Broads are special. They show how a scattered peasant population doing a normal job of work with shovels and picks can change an entire landscape over centuries. Likewise, the city is a result of a settled agriculture. Nomads graze their animals and move, and have never built a city. Without the marketable surplus of crops to make foodstuffs, urban civilisation as we know it would not exist. The sophisticated interactions of larger populations could not happen without the productivity of the farms. Without dependable rural productivity and surplus, villages could not sell to towns and merchants would be unable to transport goods for the cities in bulk. "Let them eat cakes," someone offered, *"bollocks to that,"* they said, *"give us ice cream"*.

The little coastal town of Aldeburgh is best known for its annual arts and music festival, which was founded in 1948 by the composer Benjamin Britten, his partner Peter Pears and their friend Eric Crozier. But just north of it lies the more sinister site of the twin nuclear reactors of Sizewell A and B. From near Aldeburgh you can see them both. Sizewell A is being decommissioned but during its forty year working life produced 110Twh or one trillion watt-hours of electricity, sufficient power to meet the domestic needs of England and Wales for only six months. Now, its sister reactor, Sizewell B, produces three per cent of the UK's electricity needs or roughly the equivalent of the daily domestic needs of Suffolk and Norfolk. However, Greenpeace say that this reactor produces only a paltry ten percent of what an off-shore wind farm could provide off the coast of East Anglia. How can you ride past a nuclear power station and not want to know more?

On the morning of Sunday 7th January 2007, there was an incident here which could have become a catastrophe. By chance, and very fortunately, one of the contractors working on decommissioning the Sizewell A nuclear power station was in the laundry room when he noticed cooling water leaking on to the floor. The source of the leak was from the pond that holds the reactor's highly radioactive spent nuclear fuel. It has been estimated that up to 40,000 gallons of radioactive water spilled out of a 15ft long split in a pipe, some leaking into the North Sea. The pond water level had dropped by more than a foot, yet no alarms had sounded. A report published shortly after the incident said that by the time the next scheduled safety patrol had occurred, the pond level would have dipped far enough to expose the nuclear fuel rods – potentially causing them to overheat and catch fire, so sending a plume of radioactive contamination along the coastline. If the wind had been in the right direction, this radioactive cloud would have covered London. Had that person not been in the right place at the right time, places like Aldeburgh, with its long main street of Georgian houses, it's shingle beach, independent cinema and famous Old Moot house would have become uninhabitable. Radioactive iodine would have been spread by the wind so the relevant authorities would have had to advise locals to evacuate the area immediately, or at least stuff paper under the cracks of their doors to make their house air-tight. What else, realistically, could have been done?

The report of the incident by Her Majesty's Nuclear Installation Inspectorate, was critical of the incident but supportive of the preventative measure undertaken. If the spent fuel rods had overheated, some kind of nuclear explosion theoretically could have occurred.

As the risk of annihilation that night is slim I take lodgings in the Mill Inn. The locals have started drinking early and as I dash out to take a photograph, a seagull lands nearby and a bloke shouts out, "are you going to take a picture of that seagull?"
"Come again, pal?" I said.
"That seagull that landed over there, did you go out just to take a picture of it?"
"Do you know, I've been following that one all day,"
"But how did you know it was going to land just there?" he said.
Good point.

The River Alde prevents me from continuing along the coast so I take the A1094 back to the A12 and end up on the outskirts of Ipswich. It's raining hard so I miss Felixstowe and continue on to Colchester, without sampling the joys of Harwich and Clacton-on-Sea. By Chelmsford I see no reason to visit the delights of Southend in a thunderstorm either. So goodbye Benfleet, Canvey Island and Stanford-le-Hope with my best wishes and before I know it I am riding along the northern banks of the River Thames before filtering through the Blackwell Tunnel and stopping off in Greenwich.

Whereas morsels of life in back-waters by the sea are kind and juicy, life in London can occasionally live up to the fantasy of a big city, but it can also be its antithesis. Parking by a juice bar not far from the Maritime Museum the menu advertises 101 different flavours of milkshake. It takes ten minutes to master the enormity of choice, which is ample time to have your bike nicked. The two people who run the bar, Esat and Ceylan, are from the Asian and European side of Istanbul. On the wall, posters advertise plays and jazz, jewellery makers and painters, alongside that photo from *Grease* of John Travolta and Olivia Newton-John. There was also a copy of the famous Charles Ebbets photograph 'lunchtime atop a skyscraper'; the one that shows eleven cloth-capped and fearless construction workers sitting nonchalantly on a girder 69 floors up and utterly unprotected, during the construction of a skyscraper in New York back in 1932. The reviews for local events are all spectacular, 'a life-enhancing triumph, a hot ticket ...' Why is it that I don't feel like this, not snappy, not a hot ticket? Maybe it's that chink of ordinariness which coats everything we do. John Donne once wrote that *'between that excremental jelly that the body is made of at first, and that jelly which thy body dissolves to at last; there is not so noysome, so putrid a thing in nature.'* Life is like a pure flame and whatever it's duration, it is all past in a moment.

I sit there wanting to be lazy, announcing in my head that time spent on anything you do, in the long term, doesn't really matter. Closed doors are jealous possesors of happiness, equally such existentialism is born out of an idleness which does not pay off mortgages or the hire purchase on a bike. If I am ever bored with time, as in *Waiting for Godot*, then hanging myself from a leafless willow tree would not work. Whoever said *'Money doesn't buy happiness'* doesn't know where to go shopping.

My route out to Dartford is predictably sub-urban and the first part of the A2 (which now continues as the A207) is as narrow and as busy as I remember. It was part of the Roman road to Canterbury from St Albans, which the Anglo-Saxons called Waecelinga Street and later became known as Watling Street. The old A2 is gross. It pretends to be of motorway standard when in fact there are sections that are narrow and slow. I'm on my way to Whitstable.

Off the Thanet Way in Faversham there is a small road to Graveney which leads on to Seasalter. A concrete wall separates a listless sea from a field of static caravans. Glazed-eyed blokes hang around a line of 1950s wooden sheds-for-homes. There is something 'sea shanty' about this little village that I like; it seems to cock a snook at the preciousness of 'Chelsea-by-Sea' places. Admittedly, the sea wall is a joyless appendage to the lack of imagination anyone must have to park their caravan in its shadow, and what a fruitless exercise it must be to live by the sea and not actually see it? Yet a few short bends later, Whitstable is a delight. Antiquarian bookshops, bric-a-brac and stuffed animals overflow outside cheap stores in a beguiling rather than unpleasant way. On the left up the main street, The Oyster Wheeler bar has sixteen places in the back and four in the front and epitomises the beauty of small things. Forking left to the beach I park outside the Whitstable Oyster Company, perhaps in preparation for another kip.

Green-painted window frames and shutters are encased by walls of hand-made bricks, while inside, white-painted beams support the ceiling. Paint drips have hardened down oak lintels to give the place a hand-built feel, (or maybe it was decorated by a blind painter). Whelks and cockles are £1 a pot and the half of raspberry wheat beer makes me lay my head down on the table, where, predictably I fall asleep.

People, including me, can be querulously condescending, enough to turn a showgirl into a misanthrope. As if to separate us from such foolishness maybe that is why the motorcycle helmet was invented? As soon as you put on your helmet you submerge yourself into your own personal world. Because of this I like being in my helmet, it pleasantly imprisons me with my thoughts. Keeping it on for too little a time undermines the experience and too long means you risk becoming a failed person, a believer in conspiracy theories, food fads, a person short of emotion or sense of humour, deprived of the consolations of jokes and love? After 7 circumnavigations one of the contradictions of being an isolationist in your helmet, someone who might live in an arctic wasteland, is a simple choice:

(a) stay on this planet with form-filling and 'smash-and-grab' celebrity
(b) stay in your helmet, if you have to, but at least feel superior in your strangeness!

The Ace Café had organised a gathering in Margate. Ok, so Charles Dickens and Ted Heath were connected to Broadstairs, but I wanted to go to Margate. Brit Art star Tracey Ermin came from here, and I am more drawn to a circus as it rolls into town. Bikers, big, small, fat and thin, congregate at the altar of bikeness. This journey is rapidly becoming the hardest of all to interpret.

When you ride across a sub-continent with some unfathomably complex culture, it remains just that, unfathomable. Here, everything you see is familiar and sometimes that is too much to take in.

Across from Pegwell Bay and south of Minster Marshes, I am now in Sandwich, sitting in the Fleur de Lys pub on Delf Street. It is a sunny day, and as the sun filters through the windows, prisms of colour scatter across the floor. The big old pub serves excellent breakfasts, which is much needed after sinking a few ales in the Five Bells the night before. There are shades of Eeyore (Winnie the Pooh's mate) in my head. I feel considerably less cheerful than Eeyore did when Piglet gave him a birthday present of a balloon only to fall on it and pop it, although when

Eeyore managed to fit his balloon into the honey pot he somehow made the best of a bad day and, like him, my spirits began to rise on an otherwise beautiful morning.

It occurred to me that one positive aspect of England is its benevolent and broad view of life, and this shows up in certain contrasts. In Margate, from where I have just ridden, there is a shop opposite the children's area on the beach selling ill-fitting nurses uniforms made of plastic.

Here in Sandwich, just twenty two miles away, in the main square opposite the bank, two ladies sell original Edison phonographs of the most extraordinary rarity. There is something quintessentially English about the superfluity and non-essentialness of the goods sold in both shops, even though they couldn't be more different.

Equally, there is nothing bullish in this genteel town, just people biding their time in a way of life which in some deep sense overlooks rolling downs, a sense-lulling calmness away from the jarring noise of the world. Nearby, chalk grasslands lie on the edge of ancient woodlands and it is easy to fall into a mystical dreaminess. Why not consider the importance of trees when trying to elucidate the meaning of Englishness? Things said by characters in novels somehow give an indication of how the longevity of these arboreal giants becomes a bridge across time; it gives me a sense of belonging and a sense of history. I would like to be a tree for a while: it would satisfy my need to be absorbed into the past to see if it makes some sense of the future.

After the Norman invasion of 1066 Sandwich became one of the famous Cinque Ports, with special rights and privileges, as did Dover, Hythe, New Romney and Hastings. In 1255 the first captive elephant was sailed into Sandwich Quay. A present from the French king to the English monarch Henry III it was taken on foot to the king's zoo in the Tower of London. On the way, a bull in a field approached the elephant with murderous intent (although I suppose it might have been *amour*) but was repelled with a thrust of tusk and killed outright.

Sandwich is no longer a port because the sea has retreated two miles to the east over the last seven centuries. Apart from the Royal St Georges Golf Club there is nothing but flatlands and the railway between Sandwich and the sea. The A258 takes me to Deal, a not unpleasant seaside town, and continues on to Dover. About three miles before the port that sets all motorcyclists free, I peel off left down Station Road to the Blue Bird café near St Margaret's-at-Cliffe.

The Blue Bird Café is an old coastguard station with an art deco feel to the architecture. It's obviously named after the song by Nat Burton and Walter Kent made famous by Vera Lynn during the war. *'There'll be bluebirds over the white cliffs of Dover'*.....The irony of course is that there have never been any bluebirds anywhere near Dover, a fact unknown to the American lyricist Nat Burton because he'd never been within three thousand miles of the place. Didn't stop it being a worldwide and enduring hit though!

In places like this, in what looks like a sniffy part of Kent, the clientele are all very polite and it is a super place to have a cup of tea. Mariners' trinkets sit on shelves and a blue-painted pine Welsh dresser displays a tea and cake service, a florally glazed 'Blue & White' from Crabtree and Evelyn. Jars of cakes sit on scrubbed pine tabletops and the view through windows facing the sea is of France. As I look out across the English Channel, so crisp is the light, so clear the air, I can make out individual buildings in Calais. So bright without glare, so uncluttered with any kind of foreground, the beaches off Cap Gris Nez form a thin strip of sandy brown and the cliffs of Cap Blanc Nez have a clearly defined edge backing onto fields of green and grey. A storm is coming in and as the sun strikes the ferries against a purple sky, it is like an illuminated page in an otherwise dull book.

A couple sit down next to me and a woman asks me what I am doing, and we talk about this and that, as the English do. They tell me about nearby Snowdown Colliery, how it was so hot underground, like Dante's inferno and how the miners hacked at the coalface naked except for their helmets and belts. Above ground the morphology of the landscape is similar to the chalk hills around Sandwich. Here, cropped fields of short grass roll down to a big, deciduous and very ancient looking wood. I am back to trees again because everywhere you look there usually is one. Equally, there is not a place on earth where mankind has built which does not grow a road sign; but it's not the same! 15th century English mystics saw trees as walking men, no one except drug users and drunks have made the same of a STOP sign or something that tells you to GIVE WAY! The word *'Ents'* means 'giants' in Old English and were moving trees or, less literally, the 'shepherds of the trees'. Tolkien himself describes in *The Lord of the Rings* how Ents looked like old chaps having a gathering. The concept of 'tree' is far more than the product of a lively imagination; it is intricately entwined with life itself. In the novels of Thomas Hardy, so knowledgeable were his characters that they could identify a particular species simply from the sound of the wind passing through its boughs. Moreover, that tree and that sound would manipulate a mood. In *Far From the Madding Crowd*, Hardy characterises the tree as an important part of Englishness and Britishness, going right back to Druidic, Celtic pre-Christianity. In the landscape of his humankind, it is they who *'learn how the trees on the right and the left wailed or chaunted to each other in the regular antiphonies of a cathedral choir'*.

I digress, I know. I can write about my breakfast for a chapter and how the sausages were a little under done when the bacon was actually crispy and cold. I could eulogise again over the sound of the engine and remark about those little tappets that go up and down. I could imagine what a cross-plane crank actually looked like, but it wouldn't really make any difference, it's all Chinese to me!

I get up to pay and leave. My bike stands there patiently, waiting for me. It is the sweetest thing knowing you can climb on to your bike and go wherever you want; that however long or short your time, you are incandescently free. I ride down to St Margaret's and the sea and sit in the car park adjacent to a pub at the bottom of the cliffs.

During World War II most of the population were evacuated and guns with their attendant military personnel were moved in. Most of the guns were anti-aircraft but there were smaller pieces intended to prevent German shipping from travelling along the French coast. There were two 15 inch guns called "Jane" & "Clem" and there were also the two famous ex-Navy 14-inch (356 mm) guns called "Winnie" and "Pooh" which originally came from the battleship HMS King George V. On one occasion when Winston Churchill was visiting, it is rumoured that "Winnie" was fired and the officer-in-charge saluted and reported, "a direct hit, Sir". "On what?" enquired Winston, "er – France, Sir". There was a wooden dummy of "Pooh" but it obviously did not fool the Germans as legend has it that they dropped a wooden bomb. During the war, Sir Peter Ustinov was stationed here and liked it so much he bought a house on the cliffs after the war. At the other end of the beach there are several cottages, two of which were once owned by Noel Coward and Ian Fleming.

Imagine if history could be re-written, or better still re-lived, what a future it would be? When Wilfred Owen said about the pity of war, he was talking about the trenches in World War One, about going over the top and about 'that old lie' – that it is a good and sweet thing to die fighting for your country, for good old Miss Britain. To write backwards, is an interesting thought, so that as Seamus Heaney once said, in only a slightly dissimilar way to Mark Twain how "hope and history rhyme".

My bike stands there patiently, waiting for me. It is the sweetest thing knowing you can climb on to your bike and go wherever you want; that however long or short your time, you are incandescently free.

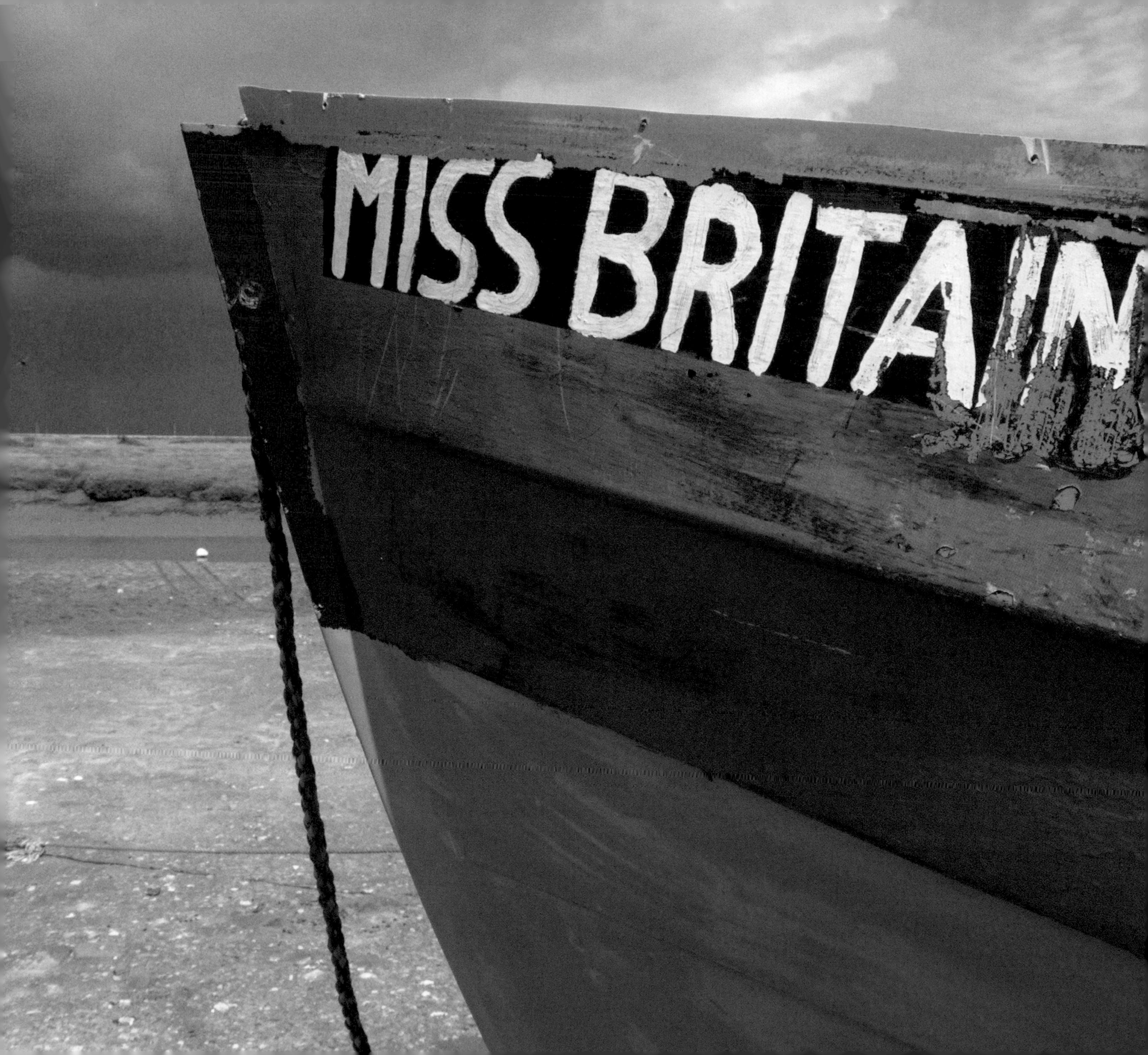
MISS BRITAIN

The bike is performing well, so well I have nothing to say, except that it is grey and pretty and judging from my Parallel World journey, it could easily be ridden across hundreds of miles of unmade African roads. It's an exceptional bike the R1, both last year's model and this new one.

Up the road in Dover a group of extreme swimmers grease themselves up to prepare for training swims in the harbour. One man, Kevin Murphy, has swum the channel 34 times and is a hero in this, perhaps the most extreme of extreme sports. Sitting with her back to the promenade wall a woman with a face the colour of a walnut keenly scans the surface of the water in the harbour. This is Frieda Streeter, the mother of channel-swimming world champion Alison, a city banker who has swum the channel no less than 43 times. Alison is Queen of the English Channel and her exploits include a triple crossing in 1990, non-stop in 34 hours 40 minutes! A feat accomplished by only three other people in the world. Her fastest and possibly most audacious swim was from France to Britain in an unprecedented 8 hours 48 minutes, followed by an equally remarkable completion of seven crossings in one year, a weather-enforced schedule prompting this hugely difficult challenge every ten days. Couldn't she have got the ferry?

On the beach I ask about the 'mental thing' but these people don't seem to know how to elaborate on the subject. I wonder if Valentino Rossi has any idea what makes him so fast. Does John McGuinness really know how he manages to lap the TT course at an average speed of over 130mph? Charlie the coach thinks swimmers get their brains a bit waterlogged; perhaps it's the same for motorcyclists?

Charlie the coach thinks swimmers get their brains a bit waterlogged; perhaps it's the same for motorcyclists?

  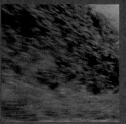 

Biking around Britain's coast is like eating all the toffees in a sweet shop until you make yourself sick. It is not a question of what to see but what can possibly be left out. My next port of call is Derek Jarman's cottage near Dungeness. Some say he was a bit bonkers, definitely gay and also a brilliant filmmaker, so that meant we possibly had at least one thing in common.

The route along the south coast is overwhelmed by a surfeit of traffic, so I get to the promontory of Dungeness with indecent haste and soon find Jarman's last home. It is a single storied cottage comprising just two small rooms. Weather-boarded on all sides, with windowsills painted yellow, it is smartly kept. In the shingle garden there are Eryngium Maritimum or Sea Holly, Poppies and sea grasses and an old lady told me that the Valerian started to bloom the day he died.

A card in the window warns people not to spy inside. I don't advocate a disregard for people's privacy but for extreme independent artists, this is the wooden equivalent of Graceland, in a wasteland, and it is of some public interest why Jarman went there to die. Like bike racers, extreme swimmers and people who live and die for what they believe in, he succumbed to his lifestyle and died overlooking a shingle beach.

The road to the house is wide enough for two cars to pass but narrows the closer you get to the notorious Dungeness nuclear power stations, less than a mile away. The Station Café, which is the terminus of the Romney, Hythe and Dymchurch railway, is so unpretentious as to be austere, while nearby, a hut selling New Age trinkets appears sensationalist and, well, just plain silly – buy an amulet and save your world.

For some, this landscape, which stretches out to a sea hidden by a horizon of pebbles, is a desert of stones.

Locals think of it differently, saying it is a unique aspect not found anywhere else in Britain. This cannot be denied and while at first I am unnerved by its strangeness, imagining a mutant species breathing in the radiation from a leaking nuclear reactor – it is not the unlikely signals of an apocalypse that I remember, it is simply a feeling which dawns on me that one day, I should like to return.

As I ride away from this strange part of Britain, a shiver of desolation descends on me. Every country I have biked through seems to have an invincible sense of identity, a hand-on-heart, hand-me-down jingoism. From India to Indonesia there are flags on the top of buildings which wave wildly in stiff breezes, whilst down at fence level, surrounding small back gardens, pots of paint decorate the landscape in their national colours. Here it is not like that and I am reminded of something Jeremy Paxman wrote about the English when he said that they 'ignore the silver lining', only to 'grasp at the cloud'. Do people believe that England is rotting because they've been told for decades that the end of empire pre-dates terminal decline?

The road from Dungeness to Rye crosses the Walland Marsh and the border from Kent to East Sussex. Historically significant tracks with names like Saxon Shore Way traverse sections of the A259. Some points of interest are easy to miss if you don't look for them on the map. Ypres Tower and Gun Gardens must carry painful memories for some people, or their descendants. Often when I look at a map of Africa and spy a village, I see a round dot that indicates a location and nothing else. Buildings are most likely built there in which people live, and a complex structure of relationships and money exist in what is otherwise ink on paper. It is obviously the same here. I see the groynes at Winchelsea and at Cliff End turn towards Hastings and Bexhill. I miss Eastbourne and Beachy Head but pause for a while in Brighton.

As you approach Brighton it has two coastal roads as you come from the east; one that hugs the promenade beside the sea and the main road higher up, which looks down on everything below. I switch from the sea road to a side road to grab a coffee and park opposite a humble-looking café called Bom-Bane's. It has a dark red frontage, yellowing newspaper clippings along the base of the window, and inside it is a cornucopia of homeliness. Jane Bom-Bane, who runs the place, has posters on the wall describing herself as a woman who *'sings as she plays her harmonium whilst wearing a mechanical hat that goes round and round'*. 'Wide-eyed and hatless, the hat lady sings' say the posters, and when the saltcellar is collected from one of the Formica-topped tables, it releases an electrical switch which in turn sets in motion musical chimes on the wall. On another table, a bearded chap, who looks as if he'd lose his footing stepping onto a pavement, is reading a book by survivalist author Ray Mears. The sun is now no longer shining on the street and shadows are creeping up the side of the buildings opposite.

I feel at home here, in this silliness. Jane rushes around the place, busying herself. The Ray Mears chap comes over and introduces himself as Dave and says goodbye and leaves. A moment later a guy with long grey hair enters the café with a delightful looking woman and suddenly the space takes on the feeling of a stage. I say hello to him and we swap greetings. He introduces himself as Paul Lewis, a composer for television who has written for Monty Python and Benny Hill. The lady with him is Sharon, a performance artist who sings while she bakes and ices cup cakes. How wonderfully odd.

Because of the proximity to each other it's difficult to separate and identify different life forms along some sections of the south coast. Littlehampton-ites dwell in a similar habitat to Rustington-ites, whilst Worthingtonions appear fused to people who lie in Goring-by-Sea. New-build has joined up these small communities so that they live along the beach like a string of pearls waiting for some traveller to pass by, such as Oscar Wilde, who wrote his play 'The Importance of being Earnest', in Worthing. I don't stop to know more and zip through Bognor Regis, Selsey Bill and East Wittering. Depending on your persuasion, cities are the fireplaces of civilization or the abyss of the human species; nevertheless, I decide on this coastal journey not to engage with big places, so pass by Portsmouth and Southampton.

A third of the way through this gentle adventure and I overtake car drivers and pedestrian tourists with just a hint of contempt, for we are bikers and not like other users of the highway. Sitting on my machine, I am a warrior of the road and slip through the New Forest to Sammy Miller's Museum at Barton on Sea.

Later in the afternoon, Sammy invites me to dinner, and along with his wife Rosemary and legendary bike builder Colin Seeley, we sit and chat. I'm embarrassed to confess that I hadn't actually heard of Colin, so quickly read about him on the internet. Between 1975 and 1978 his company was responsible for producing 300 Seeley Hondas with CB 750 engines. Most of his work, according to my reading, was sold as chassis kits into which engines were added, but Colin made his name earlier in the 1960s when he was first a Grand Prix sidecar star, then moved on to building specials powered by single cylinder 350cc AJS and 500cc Matchless engines to which he had secured the manufacturing rights. Even though I am a biker this is not a world I know a lot about, but people like Colin and Sammy, who do things in a progressive way, are of huge interest. Nothing extraordinary has ever been realised without passion and equally to be really great you have to stand with people and not above them, and this is something these men do.

Sammy sits next to his wife and across from me at dinner and Colin to my left and I want to know what it is that drives them, still, in their seventies. Sammy was eleven times British Trials Champion, twice European Champion and amongst a glittering career, winner of 1482 trials events. What truly astonished me was his ability to cross over disciplines, winning the Leinster and North West 200 Irish Road Races three years in succession. Sammy says it's all down to dedication and hard work, nothing more. Implausibly, he excludes natural talent. When others were in the pub, he was back at the beach, practising on the rocks. An hour and a half every day and if he missed one day he would do three hours the next. He refuses point blank the idea that he was a gifted individual, that he possessed some extraordinary hand-eye coordination and balance; that he was gifted with the vision of an eagle to know where to place his wheels on those crags and rocks. "When I looked at the rocks I could see every bit of detail," he said, "I knew *exactly* where I was going." Sammy's wife disagrees with him and alludes to the '*something* different' he must have had. "Don't interrupt me," he says to her, not unkindly, but when a man like Sammy is explaining something it comes with focus and has to be heard.

We talk about Joey Dunlop not retiring from racing when he should have, "but then some riders have nothing else in their lives," says Colin, (although Joey had plenty of other things in his life, from his pub to his charity drives to Romania). Still, it can be true that high achievement requires such focus, it leaves no spare time for racers to develop other aspects of their lives. "It's happening with Chris Walker and Michael Rutter; everyone has a time

when they should stop. The dangerous thing actually isn't always the riding you know," Colin continues thoughtfully, "it's the stopping."

In the car on the way home from the restaurant, Sammy drives sedately and takes the racing line but at 40mph. Colin and Sammy said their reactions are a quarter of what they were as racing men and I know too, that in the

bubble of the world of our own making, my reactions are not what they once were.

I sleep badly that night and don't know why. Halfway through the night I pick up Robert Fulton's book 'One Man Caravan' once again and select a paragraph at random. It is not what he writes about his 1930s round-the-world motorcycling that interests me as much as how I feel when I read him; he's in Arabia, *'the old man was calm enough as he paused to turn again to his water-pipe and take measured puffs. But his eyes were intense, mirroring a turmoil in his brain....what he saw I cannot say; but his next words gave an inkling of what was in his mind, if not his heart....'* With the scent of the desert in my hair I fall asleep. My dreams are of mortality and moments of finality.

The next day I have breakfast, pack and ride west. The traffic is slow, faltering behind tractors and large trucks. A depression is forming over the Irish Sea and is sweeping across Wales and Devon. The rain begins to fall heavily and there is mist over the Isle of Purbeck. From where Chesil Beach begins to form at Fortuneswell on the Isle of Portland it is barely twenty miles to Lyme Regis. I have travelled around the coast of Britain three times before this journey and every hour I am astonished at what I have forgotten and amazed at what has changed. It reminded me of a Mark Twain remark: *'history doesn't repeat itself but sometimes it rhymes'*.

"That's all the motorcycle is, a system of concepts worked out in steel."

Robert M. Pirsig

n 1996, my friend, motorcycle historian Bernd Tesch, wrote in his foreword to a new edition of Bob Fulton's 1937 book, *'One Man Caravan'*, that *'every worldwide motorcycle adventurer is unique, each with his or her own personality and each with a different dream, but when I think of Bob Fulton, I feel that his dreams have far surpassed circumnavigating the globe on a motorcycle – and, unlike most of us, he's made them all come true'*. As George Bernard Shaw said, *"You see things; and you say, 'Why?' But I dream things that never were; and I say, 'Why not?"*

In this dream-like way, people, writers, bikers like Mr Fulton blur the boundaries between history and legend. For a year and a half from July 1932 Bob travelled 25,000 miles, alone, on a Douglas Dragonfly, shooting 40,000ft of film as he rode from England to Japan. A true pioneer among biking travellers, he pushed the boundaries of how such a traveller responds to what he sees. His language is descriptive yet informative and his published work about his journey reads as well now as it must have done seventy years ago. Yet forms of language, or even concepts, don't succeed each other in neat transitions. Instead they erupt and flare and then fade away only to turn up when you least expect. Equally, as a point of reference in my own work, Fulton's book became a focus of my attention spontaneously almost mysteriously.

Such transition of a concept over time, literary or otherwise, is appropriate to any story, but perhaps most appropriate to one describing a journey. The self-determination of a motorcycle adventure is defined by freedom and allows for movement, and that is surely the physical manifestation of 'transition?' With your throw-over panniers and tank bag, GPS settings and clear intent you become part of that fanciful and fantastical kind of travel writing at which the British excel.

Extending from an oral tradition, historically the British were seen as 'seers of visions' and the Druidic priests, it's claimed, were possessed of visionary powers. In this way the earliest histories were based on visions. Serious scholars recounted visionary events soberly as acts of divine intervention, incidences that would today require a suspension of disbelief. Amazingly, there are people today and for different reasons, who could not understand a man like Fulton, have never heard of him and have no idea of the importance of what he accomplished.

There are few original thinkers and I am not one of them. When an idea or a sequence of words enters the field, it triggers a whole sentence in my head. Every thought for ordinary mortals is triggered by an action or a conversation. It could be argued that we can write nothing that hasn't already been written, that it's only a question of reassembly. According to Ackroyd, the seventh century hymn of the poet Caedmon comes up almost word for word in William Blake's eighteenth century vision in his *Songs of Innocence*.

Did Blake plagiarise Caedmon or subliminally recite it without knowing, or did he imagine it as if from some divine intervention peculiar to the fashion of the day where memory prods from angels were acceptable tools of literary function? I have drunk three coffees and slept well. It is time to leave.

The coast road from Dartmouth to Plymouth is narrow and bitty, small lanes rounding out at the edge of fields only to retrace up the other side. The low rolling hills of South Devon are in this way criss-crossed by high hedges hiding away single-tracked tarmac. High cliffs contrast with the softer beauty of tidal estuaries which themselves delve deeply inland between fields and woodlands. Just as I decided not to pass through London or Bournemouth I traverse the home of the 'sea-dogs of Devon' (Plymouth) along the A38 and two hours later I am in Truro.

The next day I am in Land's End. This is a small leap but as journeys go it is one of fancy as much as fact, and in any case, like John O'Groats, the westernmost tip of the British mainland has, even though it is visited by over one million people every year, little intrinsic significance for me.

St Ives is a compact and enchanting maze of narrow streets that all make their way to the harbour. Known as a haven for artists, visitors cram into the place like fish that have been caught in a net. As Fulton Jr, Ted Simon and other circumnavigators try to make sense of their riding, there is inevitably ruin in the plan. It's hard to go away and it's hard to return home. At least as bikers we do not flood into honey pot places and get our boots stuck in the mud. There is something about the lemming nature of the tourist that doesn't know how to deal with space. It's like they follow each other around, as if afraid to be alone, terrified of getting lost. It is a world within which a missed bus becomes a crises. As a biker, you just get on your bike and leave. The motorcycle may only be a system of 'concepts worked out in steel' but it digs deeply into the soul of the rider. Walking around from café to burger bar is a test of patience but riding your bike functions as a process of reason.

So I climb on my bike and ride, past Newquay and Padstow, small bays, big bays, Tintagel Head and Boscastle, on beyond The Strangles and more grim beauty carved by the sea before I settle somewhere for the night.

The typical peasant village before the enclosures was one of people working together on communal land. Surrounded by open arable strips and unfenced pasture land where stock was herded. With the enclosures at the end of the 18th century, the landscape changed from a flat, bare look to one of being dressed with ditches, or where stone was available, dry stone walls or earthen banks known as 'baulks' in the West Country but hedgerows were commonly planted everywhere. Each system was used as a way of controlling the movement of once herded cattle. In 1978 there were 600 000 miles of hedges in Britain, and if they averaged 2ft wide that was an area larger than all the then designated nature reserves. Without the hedgerow the once open landscape looked souless and bleak but then unlike now there existed vast swathes of natural forest which have since been hewn.

Walking around from café to burger bar is a test of patience but riding your bike functions as a process of reason.

My temporary ownership of the 2009 R1 is over. After a service by Laurie, Webb's chief mechanic in Eye near Peterborough, I am back on the 2007 bike that took me around my Parallel World. The hard ride across the Nubian and Didu Gagalu Deserts had only marked the machine superficially. New panels have been sprayed in Carole Nash blue, and the headstock fairing support that was broken during transit from the Port of Newark, New Jersey to Southampton Docks, is fixed and now supports a new screen. This recycling of a motorcycle with 38,000 miles on the clock is a perfect testimonial to a bike that did more miles in six months than most people do in ten years. It's still barely a year old and it still goes like stink.

We, the circumnavigators, are people who go around things. I am not sure if it is our job to make sense of this; to know why we push though the normal consensus of what is thought to be reasonable. I think it has nothing to do with being reasonable. Film director Clint Eastwood said, "I tried being reasonable, I didn't like it". Reasonable people adapt to the world they are in, unreasonable people expect the world to change with them. As Shaw said, 'all progress depends on the unreasonable man.'

"Most motorcycle problems are caused by the nut that connects the handlebars to the saddle."

Anon

In Borth, gradually rising sea levels at the end of the ice age would have been comparable to the deluge story of Noah's Ark, where God sends down a flood to destroy the earth. Practically, the remains of a sunken forest could be associated with some great tragedy, which had overcome a community long ago, and the nourishment of myth is grown from that. Beneath the beaches and the Welsh stones there are treasures, layered with lead and gold, manganese, iron ore, copper, tin and coal. The Celts used to sink deep shafts to reach the earth-gods and Welsh folklore is full of stories of the nether world and some hidden middle-earth. Mysteriously, but possibly unifying fact with fiction, in 1770 a Welsh antiquarian scholar William Owen Pughe made it known that he had seen sunken human habitations four miles off the Ceredigion coast between the rivers Ystwyth and Teifi. That evening I ride into Machynlleth. The road is smooth but winds. I eat a fish supper at Dick's Diner and while the chips are hot I had to ride through downpours of biblical proportions to get them. Yet, over the nearby hills a shaft of sunlight catches the rain and it looks like a trapdoor to heaven.

The next day, in my charming home town of Machynlleth, I sit in the Quarry café. It is a vegetarian restaurant with a preference for mung bean salads, home made pizzas and filled potatoes. Paradoxically, it's situated next to a butcher's, and it's a pleasing fact that during student vacations, their serving staff are sometimes the prettiest this side of the border. Coffee over, no need to snooze, so I turn right at the clock tower and cross the bridging point of the Dovey. Left after the bridge and the road follows the river, winding through Pennal, Cwrt and the edge of Happy Valley before the start of the estuary. On a summer's evening when the shadows are long and the tide recedes to expose small dunes, if you squint, it's like looking over the Sahara.

The road out of Aberdovey passes the golf club on the left and further up, the cemetery on the right. It continues through Tywyn and a few minutes later, a small unmarked road bears off to the left signposted for Tonfanau. The Crewe and South Cheshire Motor Club are holding one of their events at the small circuit by the cute little railway station overlooking the sea. The sheep muck has been scraped off the track and everyone is ready to race. Rain clouds sit out in the bay and threaten a downpour but instead behave

themselves and dump their load where they are and do not venture inland. I stay a while then continue. Around about little roads here are never straight, instead they tumble through fields of brown and green, across contours that naturally fall to the sea.

M.HAILWOOD

HONDA

10

A touch further north, the village of Penmaenpool is at the head of the Mawddach Estuary and is centred around a wooden planked toll bridge and the George III Hotel. The area is said to be one of the most beautiful in Europe. The hotel has a Dresser Bar overlooking the bay and I see houses dotted about the hillside, half hidden in a swath of impenetrable coniferous forest. Cumulus clouds have grown all morning and the forecast is for thunder, but all that can be heard is the sound of loose planks on the nearby bridge, underneath the weight of passing cars.

The bar operates on what looks like a chest of drawers and something about the atmosphere feels 'untouched'. The mixture of church pews and line drawings of the estuary are punctuated by an assortment of brass plates fixed to a stone wall. It's not that what happens is not important enough to be noticed in places like this, simply, it has to be seen in the first place.

Further up the river, Dolgellau is situated on the confluence of the Arron and the Wnion, and both these small rivers are joined a few hundred yards to the west by more small tributaries trickling down the south facing slopes of Mount Snowdon.

The toll bridge at Penmaenpool crosses the Mawddach but the more established head of the estuary is Dolgellau just a few minutes ride back down the road. On the way in to this pleasant but slightly austere Welsh town, I enter Eldon Square where there is a newsagent on the corner and buses stand on the left, presumably a terminus for passengers before restarting their journey.

Opposite the Royal Ship Hotel, Robert's Café immediately strikes me as having that rare charm of a coffee house being run well. The deep mauve windowsills are rich and commanding, encompassing 48 panes of glass either side of a centrally located door. A beautifully worked counter sits the full depth of the interior and is a remnant from when the building was used as an ironmonger's. It stands on land once occupied by the ancient Parliament of Wales. There is a dispute as to whether Glyndŵr's court was here or in Machynlleth, but seated underneath oil-lit chandeliers, the timelessness of the coast makes an impression on me once again.

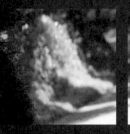
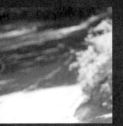

Getting to know a place is only partly to do with liking it. Journalist Simon Jenkins in his book *'Wales, Churches, Houses, Castles'* says that, *"by the middle of the century the story of Welsh buildings is of a country that appeared to have lost identity and heart."* Not only did the planning for individual buildings suffer, the quality of urban planning was dreadful. He goes on to say, *"Wales is the world capital of the self-deprecating remark,"* and when I see ruinous-looking slum estates in the south and north, sporadically planted within sight of extraordinary town houses built in a different age, you have to ask where does it come from, this visual defeatism in a land of such extraordinary natural beauty? Jenkins quotes the artist Kyffin Williams talking about an innate Welsh desire for *"the seam of melancholy that is in most Welshmen and that derives from the dark hills, the heavy clouds, and the enveloping sea mists."*

It would seem that even a knowledgeable Welshman like Jenkins, (who has a house in London and another in Aberdyfi), is as baffled by Welshness as anyone. Like me, sitting on my bike watching the sea and turning my head to see the hills, I am also enchanted. I love this place. I adore the mystery and the oddness of it. *"The English are starkly ignorant of Wales,"* he writes and that is it. Wales has remained Welsh because apart from holidaying in Porthmadog, Llandudno and Rhyl, most English don't seem that interested in it. In Barmouth, Forget-me-Knot card shops, Fat and Skinny Buddha shops, Snips and Clips and beauty parlours called Shady Eyes follow the seaside postcard habit of naming shops in the style of parody. This chases the curve of the Kingdom by the Sea from Brighton to Barmouth and back. Looking out to sea is always more spiritual than looking onto the land. The sea is impervious to the kind of change expressed on land. It can be hard to look at the beauty of edifices, you feel pre-emptively sad knowing a freshly decorated building will eventually decay. Out there, boats sit quietly like coloured sweets, all tidy and with the suggestion of somewhere new to go. Towns on the coast by definition do not have this sense of movement, just litter bins of lolly wrappers and fat people eating far more than is good for them.

On the way to Harlech I stop my bike outside a SPAR grocer's because a sign advertises the establishment as being the champion sausage maker in North Wales. In Celtic mythology, the pig was an influential animal in the underworld and the first President of the National Welsh Pig Society, founded in the 1930s, informed the world that, 'there is no breed of swine older and purer than ours'. I bought a sausage and then rode on. The coast of Britain is so dense a jungle of incredible things, of monuments and people, birds of prey and paradise and ridiculous moments of architectural splendour, it is sometimes impossible to build up a rhythm on the bike. One mile before Harlech I turn off the main road and motor down a side road winding through gardens and bungalows until once again the bike is rested in a 'display and pay' car park. Through an adjacent gate, tucked deeply into the sand dunes that separate it from the sea, lies one of the oldest little Christian churches in the world.

The coast between the Dovey and Artro estuaries is one long sandy shore supported in the background by Cader Idris and the Rhinog mountains. Neat stone-built villages connect up the coast road making this a very elegant part of the journey.

After three days in the rain, riding from Blackpool to Girvan and managing to stay upright, an extraordinary light begins to reflect off dark clouds. In the harbour two men fillet wormy looking things and across the way, The Harbour Fish Restaurant has a place set for my fish tea. Having washed down chips with a cuppa and because all the rooms around Troon and Ayr are filled with golfing enthusiasts I veer off for Kilmarnock. It is the Open and Tiger Woods is teeing off all week. There are no youth hostels, even though I am not a youth, but bed and breakfast accommodation is universally more expensive because of the influx of visitors. In the heart of the town, the Portman Hotel looks careworn and friendly but is full. They suggest the Broomhill Hotel up the road; turn right at the floral display by the station and on the right along the London Road. It is equally careworn but the owner has a room and a place for my bike. The room is borderline sad but buoyed amazingly by the warm hospitality and it's perfect for my cheap needs.

The next morning I notice my chain has lengthened, again. After tightening it, I call a dealer in town to have a new one fitted. Jimmy is the mechanic and once worked the doors in the city when gangsters ruled nearby Glasgow. He had short hair, tattoos – nothing new there then – and looks like a thousand hard men you might meet on your travels. Jimmy puts my bike on a stand, grinds off the heads of two pins from one of the chain's sideplates then drapes it on the swinging arm. Tea break. Sitting outside with his fellow mechanic he starts his tea break during which he smokes four cigarettes and then tells me he has terminal cancer. He says that he does not know how long he has got but that some kind of redemption is called for. Bowel cancer that, as he says, 'could spread like a dandelion in a gust of wind', and he uses his hand as if to blow a kiss. At the age of forty this man has a young son whom he lives for yet he goes back to the bike and continues working on it.

He asks me what it's like to travel alone and I tell him. "Na' me," he said, "They'd be that many black bastards wig guns." I say it isn't about the colour, I tell him it is about the power. If they kill me, no one would come looking, and no one would ask any questions. "Yaw right there mi son", he said, "ye woodnae get me on ma bike there, no way. Ma idea of a holiday is Ibiza; bar…pool…bar…club…beach…bar". He pauses, and feeds the new chain through the front sprocket. Quiet for a few moments, nothing is said when suddenly he starts, *"Ha' ye heard of Errol Hick?"* I hadn't, but I couldn't quite catch what he said. *"It's a character on television and he's bin a bad boy an' is seekin' to make amends for all his bad deeds. He's goin' back thru his life to make things bitter, an' I am doin' tha same thing,"* he paused, *"but nae wi' the ex-wife,"* and he winks. *"A ha' bin bad and I wan' tae make certain things right before ah go, ye ken?"* I did and told him so. *"Ah sat wi' gangstas wi' guns an' they're off tha heid wi' cocaine an' ya never ken wha' happens next".* I sit there, just listening. As a traveller, you become a conduit for other people's stories. The story man is safe, because the idea of a 'tough man seeking redemption' is a modern fable, and when told to a traveller it is taken far away and doesn't come back to haunt the teller. It's like opening your heart to a secret tree; to a special one that knows not to tell a tale.

That afternoon I ride on through Glasgow and towards the Highlands. Suddenly, after taking five weeks to get here from Hunstanton to the mountains the big space finally beckons. I take the motorway out to the Erskine Bridge across the Clyde to Old Kilpatrick and then northwest for Dunbarton and the A82 along the western shore of Loch Lomond. It is easier to divert from the coast so as to simplify my route through the glens. Magically, the buildings have largely gone and I am on wide sweeping bends funnelled through forests of coniferous trees. The city, with its stink and noise, no longer exists except as a memory. Here, taking a left for Garelochhead, the bike begins to make its familiar purr and flicks around ever tightening corners and hammers along the straights. Ahead, the horizon is blocked by billowing clouds. If it were just me and the bike, it would not be necessary ever to go home. In fact, home would no longer be a place, but wherever I happened to be at that moment.

Tyndrum is only 60 miles from Glasgow but feels on the edge of another world. Dominated by the Green Welly Café, bikers by the dozen turn up and leave in the time it takes to fuel up. That night I stay in a bunkhouse up the road behind the Bridge of Orchy Hotel. The man in my bunkroom is a walker and the stench from his socks is excruciating. I ask him to throw them out of the window and he does. The next day I ride towards Glencoe and turn off to the Clachaig Inn down a narrow side road to the right. There is a sign on the reception desk which says 'No Hawkers or Campbells'. It is raining and there is low cloud. I plod on and think. As you look up and down the U-shaped valley you see no escape. Its history is intense.

As part of the subjugation of the Highlands after the collapse of the Jacobite rising of 1689–90 when trying to return the Stuarts to the throne, a royal order required all clan chieftains to take an oath of allegiance to King William and Queen Mary. The chief of the MacDonalds of Glencoe did so but only after being purposefully delayed so missing the time limit of 1 January. Sir John Dalrymple, the Scottish Secretary used this late compliance as an excuse to send a company of Campbells, hereditary enemies of the MacDonalds, to forcibly deal with the issue. After being given traditional Highland hospitality, on 13 February 1692. The massacre began simultaneously in three settlements along the glen - Invercoe, Inverrigan, and Achnacon – and thirty-eight MacDonalds from the Clan MacDonald of Glencoe were killed by the guests who had accepted their hospitality. Another forty women and children died of exposure in the bitter winter weather after their homes were burned. Interestingly, other members of the invading company decided to forewarn their hosts and two lieutenants, Farquhar and Kennedy, actually broke their swords rather than carry out their orders. More detachments were sent to converge on the escape routes, but be it bad weather or disillusionment with what under Scottish law is known as 'murder under trust' – the most heinous kind – the men arrived late to prevent further blood being spilled. It was the *'Mort Ghlinne Comhann',* the Murder of Glencoe.

Where Loch Leven joins Loch Linnhe, I turn north to Fort William or *An Gearasdan,* as its known in Scots Gaelic. At the station, it's 10.25 and the Jacobite locomotive is steamed up and pulling away on the West Highland line which runs from here to Mallaig, This route is known as the finest railway journey in the world, supposedly better even than the line to Machu Picchu in Peru or the Siberian Express. How its wheels would clatter you to a hypnotic sleep and the roll of the carriages sedate you. I would have swopped my R1 for that train just then but instead I take the A82 along Loch Lochy past the Wells of the Seven Hearts and west onto the A87 through the Beinneun Forest on the north shore of Loch Cluanie. It's still raining and when it stops, trees that form a canopy overhead here continue to rain and prevent any sun and wind from drying the road.

It is said that impatience is good, only when it is the shortest way to get to where you need to be, otherwise patience is best and after a few more miles of wiggling and winding I am at the start of the climb to Applecross. Known in English as the 'Pass of the Cattle' it rises from sea level at the Applecross side to the summit of 626 metres. It's one of the few highland roads engineered and laid down in the style of the great mountain passes of the Alps and with tight hairpin bends at the top and gradients of 20%, it claims the steepest prolonged ascent of any road in Britain.

At the bottom of the pass the clouds ahead are menacing but blue sky begins to carve up the darkness and at the top the sun is shining. The *Bealach na Ba* is not so moody today. It is an easy ride but gravel in the centre of a track narrower than a bike length slows down movement on the bends. The sound of the bike echoes against the sides of the pass making tight metallic components clatter against precipices and boulders and beneath a darkening sky.

Normally there is accommodation in Applecross but no longer. Everything is booked throughout the summer. Thanks to a recent TV series its fame is strangling its famed sense of isolation so this time it is time to go back the way I came.

Back at the bottom of the pass I turn left towards Shieldaig. This is a single-track road and I fly along it. The bike skits on the bumpy surface and it's like dancing. Robert Dunlop and Mr McGuinness do this ever so much better on the TT course but what I can I do and like wings unfurling in a breeze, everything happens in split-second judgements; a pull, more pulling hard, a minute correction, quickly twisting, a lean, up and faster, opening up the throttle trying to get very fast, then brake, too much, then round and on through the Glenshieldaig Forest. On the left the small summit of An Staonach is dressed in heather while hill-tops further away are a blur as the road and the mountainside becomes one. Nearby I notice the yellow tops of Scottish primrose next to bluebells and fields of bracken. I try to capture the sight of anything quickly but apart from snatches of colour everything rushes past. In the bottom of the valley there is a burn that will flow to fill a loch, and in the distance small buildings rapidly close in as the sound of my fast engine, breaking through the wind, is sucked silent, until the wind changes once again and is then broken by small voices.

The next day I ride 30 miles from the village of Shieldaig to its namesake, also confusingly called Shieldaig. I cannot think of anywhere in the country where there are two places with the same name so close together; as the crow flies they're less than fifteen miles apart, although it's more like thirty miles by road. Apparently the name means 'Herring Bay' in Old Norse, but these are two different bays.

Bearing east from the village of Torridon I turn my back on the Pass of the Winds *(Bealach na Gaoithe)* and the hill Beinin Alligin, slowly weaving through the Torridon and Flowerdale Forests and along more single track destitution roads which in this case follow burns in the shadow of ranges of red sandstone. The name 'Destitution Road' is a reminder of a grim piece of Scottish history. In 1846 the potato crop was blighted in the Highlands, just as it was in Ireland the year before. This led 1.7 million people to leave Scotland over the next six years. Known as The Highland Potato Famine, it caused crippling hardships to these 19th century crofters as the potato was the only crop that could be grown in such harsh conditions. Oatmeal and other supplies were distributed in famine relief programmes that became semi-permanent. The daily ration was set at 24 ounces (680 g) per man, 12 oz (340 g) per woman and 8 oz (230 g) per child and meagre though they were, these food rations were not free as the crofters were expected to do a full week's work building roads locally, and so these became known as 'destitution roads'.

The next day I ride along the shores of Loch Ewe, which lies close to the same latitude as Labrador and Leningrad and the only soil is acid peat. Yet the North Atlantic Drift that gives the coasts of Ireland and Scotland their humid and mild weather does encourage plants to grow. After the tiny village of Poolewe (one post office, one bistro café, one hotel), Osgood Mackenzie's transformation of a barren peninsula of red sandstone is complete; it is an oasis of colour. Known as Inverewe Gardens, it consists of two thousand acres of Monterey pines, eucalyptus, hydrangea, rhododendrons and exotic shrubs from around the world. If there is yet another road that must count as one of the most scenic in the world it is this, the A832, specifically from Kinlochewe to Gairloch and over the Red Point Peninsula (Rubha Reidh).

Just spitting distance from Bad Bog there is the easily-missed village of Aultbea. I follow a dead end track, along the bank of Loch Ewe to Mellon Charles and find a café that makes and sells perfumes. Looking out from here, light reflects off the water's surface; it gives the edge of small surf an almost electric clarity and it presents a stage for Scotland's highest mountain range, the Torridons. Here, in a wind that can topple trees (or at least bend big branches), grey seas are flecked by waves racing in through The Minch from Harris and Skye.

Ullapool is pretty but full of tour buses. It's the end of the line for the faint-hearted because to go further north is to commit to a process of such beauty it will overwhelm you. At the harbour, the fishing boats are mooring. Two German riders on Indian bikes pull up and we chat. They are riding to an Indian motorcycle rally near Edinburgh later in the week. I leave the town and head north on the A835, turning left towards the Aird of Coigach. Here you look for a right hand turn for Lochinver and continue along what is a single track road with passing places. Craggy outcrops of granite are covered with white patches of lichen while small pale white air plants, skeletal and spongiform like coral, sit on rocks and at the base of purple heather. I sit overlooking a lochan (a small loch), its water lapping gently, a rowing boat loosely tied to a tree. Ferns are everywhere and flap in a warm breeze. Here, on the edge of the Celtic Rain Forest, rocks, walls and trees are covered with white and grey fungus. If you scratch beneath the surface the colour changes to reveal blue-green algae sandwiched in between the fungal surface and the rock.

Along narrow roads that follow every bump and contour, the riding can never be in a straight line. Not for a tyre's width does the track extend to any kind of horizon, instead booting you around corner to bend and back. I am approaching Durness and the cul de sac to Cape Wrath stretches away to my left while inland lies one of the largest expanses of uninhabited land in Britain. South west of the Cape, the highest cliffs on the British mainland culminate in *Cléit Dhubh* – the Black Cliff – which rises 850ft sheer from the sea. Here the sea pounds the coast with an almost unimaginable relentlessness and in deep winter on a stormy night, life in the lighthouse must be drawn from a mindset that is as special as it is isolated.

As you ride into Durness there's a petrol station on the right and a provisions store on the left, behind is the dead-end road to Balnakeil and ahead, a group of bikers were drinking tea in front of the second of the two stores. This was their big holiday of the year, blighted by the fact that two of them snored. Biker A and Biker B had just had a 'snore-off' whereby the one who can't stand it any longer goes to sleep in the corridor. Biker A says that he sounds like a seal in pain and that when he starts, his wife moves out of the house. If ever he turns up the volume a bit, his wife suggests he goes for a weekend away on his bike, which he does, about twenty six weekends a year.

Quickly shifting through the gears, ready for more single-track riding, I bike out of Durness but suddenly stop at Smoo Cave. Located at the eastern edge of the village, just off the A838 road to Tongue, the cave is set into limestone cliffs at the head of a narrow inlet. Two hundred feet long, one hundred and thirty feet wide and fifty feet high at the entrance, Geodha Smoo is the largest coastland cave in Britain and runs inland for six hundred feet.

According to 'Scottish Witchcraft Lore' by Alexander Polson (born in 1777), the cave was formerly believed to be the abode of spirits who guarded this entrance to the nether world. The first Lord of Reay (Donald Mackay, Chief of Clan Mackay) met with the Devil on several occasions and was able to get the better of him. The Prince of Darkness was none too pleased about this and followed Donald Mackay to Durness where he sought to waylay him in Smoo Cave. Lord Reay was heading for the cavern just before dawn but had the good fortune to send his dog into the blackness in front of him. When the animal came out howling and hairless the master of Reay realised what lay in store for him. He held back for a moment and in that moment the sun rose. In the light of day, the Devil was powerless and left through the roof of the cave leaving the three holes seen today.

There is a local legend about a feared highwayman, Donald McMurdo (aka Domhnull MacMhurchaidh). In the early seventeenth century, this hired assassin murdered eighteen victims by throwing them down the blowhole into the cave. In the dead of night, McMurdo would turn up in his black cape and swoop on an unsuspecting traveller and hurl his screaming victim into the abyss of Smoo. Take yourself back to the 1600s, when by a coast of thrashing winds and wild seas; it was a wet, dark land of peat and sinking bog. The only way across was on horseback along a solitary and treacherous trial.

A mile before Durness there is a church at Balnakeil and marked on the outside south wall there is a plaque that reads DMMC 1623. This is the resting place of McMurdo who, so terrified was he of being buried in unconsecrated ground, paid the church a thousand pounds to be allowed sanctuary on his death.

A thousand pounds was a king's ransom four hundred years ago and to illustrate this by comparison it was in October 1598 when Richard Quiney of Stratford, whose son married one of William Shakespeare's daughters, wrote to the Bard asking him for a loan of thirty pounds. In 1598, this sum was the equivalent in today's money of £15,000. Extrapolating from these figures to the £1000 gift supposedly given by McMurdo to the church twenty five years later, it would have to be multiplied by 500, which would make it the equivalent of half a million pounds today!

Around this time, the illegal practice of working small stills in the district of Durness, specifically in the vicinity of Smoo Cave, was carried out in regular and uninterrupted fashion. When Customs and Excise Officers came to appropriate alcohol-making equipment and exact fines, they would be lured into the cave, their boat overturned and they'd be drowned.

Centuries on, the highway across this district of Sutherland is still only the width of one car, with regular passing places. And it's thin too; it feels like a single layer of asphalt that sweeps across menacing moors, in one of the most isolated areas of Europe. This region has the lowest population density of anywhere in the United Kingdom, less than the vast pampas of Argentina, less than Papua New Guinea and such desolation matches the spirit of the dark clouds that are rolling down from the mountains today.

Accumulating from the south, a front is building and speckles of fine rain start to land on my visor. The narrowness of the track competes with its rough surface for my immediate attention, as sheep litter the boundary between what is hard and soft. Riding here at speed is a bit like the closed public roads racing they do in Ireland and the Isle of Man, but not as fast! You pretend to be Cameron Donald or Joey Dunlop, one of the Armoy Armada. As you brake hard into corners, the track twists and pitches to form blind horizons across a landscape as old as time itself. You ride across it as fast as you dare. Instead of recognising faces in the crowd as those crazy racers sometimes do, short wiry grasses flash past, but it is the heather with purple flowers that catches the corner of your eye. At the bottom of Loch Eriball, the road turns back up the other side to skedaddle across the A'Mhoine plateau on the Kyle of Tongue before shooting rapidly over the causeway.

The world's most northerly palm tree grows in Tongue, but hey, so what? I fire up out of the village and into more rain. The A838 has turned into the A836 and I ride from Coldbackie to Borgie, steaming into a hotel car park like a sweaty horse.

The village of Bettyhill is named after Elizabeth, Countess of Sutherland, the wife of the Duke of Sutherland, who was responsible for evicting 15,000 people during the time of the clearances. Some of her former tenants, brutally cleared from their crofts, were resettled here and Bettyhill became a refugee camp for people who had everything taken from them and nowhere, realistically, to go. If the geomorphology of the area is anything to go by, you begin to recognise a landscape that is the oldest in the world. It is a Cambrian and pre-Cambrian landscape containing smaller formations of Lewisian gneiss nearly three *billion* years old. Living here as a settler in mid-winter with only rocks and straw for shelter, must have been like living at the beginning of time.

The hotel brochure says *'excellent Scottish cuisine'* but the reality is an over-baked steak pie and burnt peas. The brochure tells of *'friendly Scottish hospitality'*, but what you get is a surly waitress from Monrovia and someone from Poland on reception. Yet, outside, there is a sunset deepening into such beauty, that it makes your heart beat slower.

The next day I ride to John O'Groats. The great highlands have flattened to become plains, and the majesty of the mountains is no more. John O'Groats is scruffy and pitiful. It is a sad place where great people end or start great things. I wonder why I am here and quickly leave.

As a traveller, your service to mankind is as a source of income to merchants and hoteliers. Travelling anonymously you are in every other way an invisible freak from another kingdom. You don't know anyone and you view people with trepidation. They look at you with suspicion and watch for weaknesses. It is easier without people.

Looking out of another hotel window in yet another village, I see a little red door across the road. It is positioned on the gable end of a row of houses with small windows and curtains. What happens behind that door? What is it you get to know when you pass by a place like this and stay the night? Mrs MacKay could be seeing the handsome man at the butcher's, when her husband's away, and there are funny goings on at the church ('warden nicks coffers'), and Mrs Baxter makes it her business to know why Mrs McCreedy pops over to see the chap on the end, the moment his wife takes the children to school.

The Portman Arms in Lybster has been a coaching inn for two hundred years. It quietly watches the life in this village. Vividly, carefully, lovingly and licentiously through its windows, its guests also contribute to the oral history of this small community. Stories which by definition must be based on misinterpretations and gossip. The next morning you check out of your hotel and the whole process of guesswork and voyeurism starts again, but in a different place.

Towering cliffs climbing to the 750ft Ord of Caithness are one of the most impressive features of this part of the coast. Neat Victorian villages cluster around busy working centres and are punctuated by perfect examples of sheltered deserted coves. It's a wild shoreline down to Inverness and only a little less so further east and then south to Aberdeen. The wind roughs up a grey surface into flakes of white surf and once again it rains. All day dark clouds drop their loads and all day the sound of my R1 purrs and strobes its hum against things that make sound bounce.

I turn off the A90 into Stonehaven and continue on the A92 coast road to Montrose and Arbroath, both names made familiar to me as a child listening to the television and the Saturday afternoon football results. As ever, with all of my journeys it is with a mixture of nostalgia and a need to return home that I decide to quicken my pace. The route down to Edinburgh is without incident and further around the Firth of Tay, St Andrews and the Firth of Forth I am suddenly in the city itself.

South of Edinburgh at Traquair House, Indian Motorcycle enthusiast Alan Forbes has organised a rally and people from all over the world have shipped their machines to be there. I love Indians and found time to gen up on the history of the marque.

A man called George Hendee founded The Indian Motorcycle Company in 1901 but unlike his great rivals, Messrs Harley and Davidson, he immediately looked to Europe for sales and sporting success. The year before the Great War of 1914-18, for instance, O C Godfrey raced his Indian to victory in the Isle of Man TT and the three-man Indian team won the Scottish Six Days Trial, the world's toughest. That same year, the company introduced its 1,000cc, V-twin, sport-tourer

at the London Show. It cost £77 but its specification included all-chain drive, superior trailing link front and swinging fork rear suspension, all-electric lighting from a dynamo powerful enough to balance its lighting load at a mere 8mph in top gear, a tough two-speed gearbox and clutch and a robust frame supporting a fully sprung pillion seat. It even had electric starting! The motorcycle press raved; *Motor Cycling* called it "Supersensational". By comparison, Triumph's rival and highly regarded, single-cylinder 4 horse power model clearly reflected its bicycle-based pioneering origins and still cost £63.

In 1927 Indian took over manufacturing rights of the famous but bankrupt ACE company's 1,265cc in-line four, which had been designed by Bill Henderson, who previously had produced his own in-line four. As the 90mph Indian 4 model, the uniquely civilised ex-ACE motorcycle set transcontinental record-breaking standards of endurance and reliability. It was the equal of anything then available. Sadly Indian, like Britain's BSA-Triumph and then Norton Villiers Triumph collapsed not so much from competition but more from the consequences of plain bad management. The last ones were built in the early 1950s.

Around me were a clutch of excellent machines and I felt distinctly out of place on a modern sportsbike. After some time spent perusing the assembled classics I left for Northumberland.

ENGLAND

Born in the seventh century, the Venerable Bede was spotted by an important monk as a seven year old lad bright enough to memorise the Latin psalmody and hymnal. Suffering from a speech impediment he was cured whilst researching the life of St Cuthbert. The young *oblate* was transferred to Jarrow monastery where he was to spend the rest of his life. He was a deacon at nineteen and an ordained priest at thirty. At the close of his great work, the *Historia Ecclesiastica Gentis Anglorum*, he admitted in a short autobiographical passage that he had laboured in his cell for some thirty years, writing sixty-eight books. These included commentaries on Mark and Luke, histories of the saints and all researched and written without moving an inch outside of his 10 foot square cell of stone separated within by a wooden screen set aside for prayer.

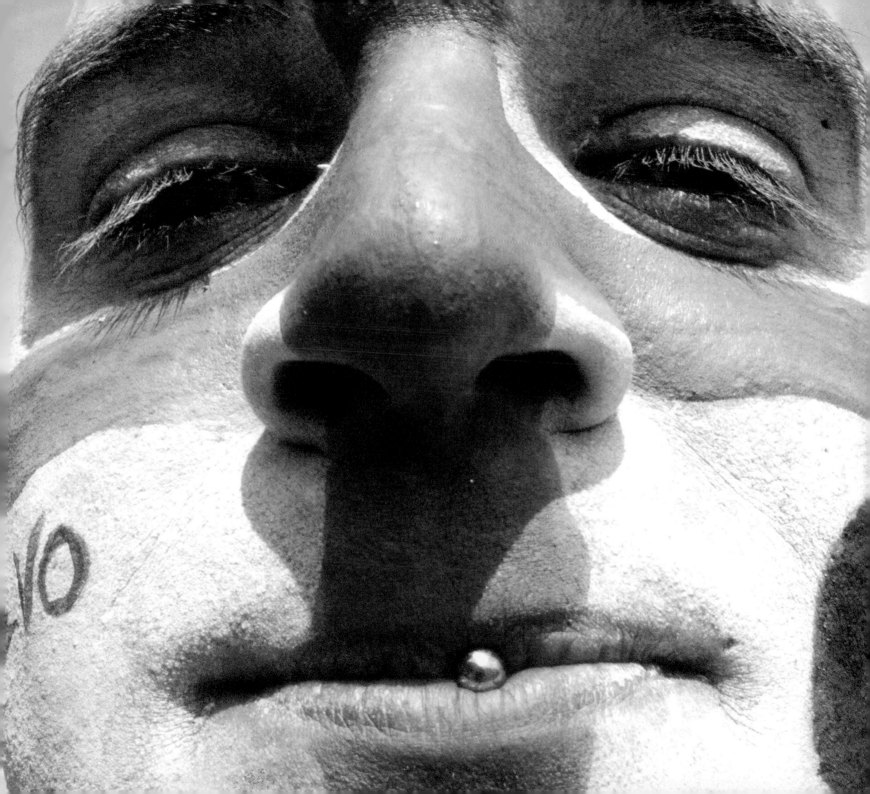

Bede himself was often visited by angels and eleven hundred years later so was the visionary poet William Blake. It has been commented that perhaps they were the same ones. Dreamers of the Anglo-Saxon tribes were praised in the charmed sleep-state. The Knights of King Arthur pursued a Holy Grail and the less fictional King Alfred dreamt of muses and heros that would guide him to victory.

Visitations are a kind of realism which we, in a world preoccupied by the need for proof, find hard to understand. It is a world, or 'non-world', that has a relevance only to those who believe in dreams being real. A monk named Drylhelm, also from Northumbria, was escorted by an angel to a *very broad and deep valley of infinite length* where the condemned souls of the departed were tossed in fire. And yet having had a conversation whilst bathing in water with blocks of ice he said, *'I have known it colder'*. Even in the 'non-world' it has been said that understatement is a British national trait.

Weather, religion and property were three important characteristics that put meat on the bone of what might be thought an important national quality, characterised by how the English, or British, see themselves. The second world war is littered with durable myths of embattled persecution, sacrifice against the odds and a level of exaggeration that war tends to propagandise. War gives people a common purpose and the British are perculiarly good at it. Religion of course can have the same effect. The first book of John Foxe's Book of Martyrs appeared in 1563 and seven years later had expanded to 2,300 pages of gory text detailing the Roman Catholic persecution of English Protestants in the reign of 'Bloody Mary'. England had become Protestant under Henry VIII (simply so he could divorce Catherine of Aragon to marry Anne Boleyn). Then his daughter Mary, married to Philip of Spain, tried to make it Catholic again before Anne's daughter Elizabeth made it Protestant once more when she came to the throne in 1558, on Mary's death. Foxe's work was displayed in churches across the country to be read by literates and also to the uneducated. Pregnant women were burnt at the stake, their stomachs exploding out newborn babies, only for them to be thrown back onto the fire as martyrs. This reign of terror was a religious civil war but it became part of the defining process of what makes up a national characteristic.

Sitting in a Travel Lodge not far from Berwick, I have little to do other than read. Whilst religion is one vital process in understanding who we are, property is another. It is the English, and in this case equally prevalent in Scotland and Wales, that the ownership of a house makes it difficult to properly meet an English person. Riding my bike along the byways of the coast of Britain it is unusual to reasonably gain access to what he or she is thinking. If I ask a biker why he rides his bike he will say because of the freedom it allows and the exhilaration of being at speed on the open road. If someone on the street is asked what it means to be English, he or she might talk about red telephone boxes and cricket and other obvious 'afternoon tea and scones' stereotypes that amazingly still persist.

It is the 'American in England' who announces the fact that it is hard to make friends with the English. That they do not care very much to belong. They hardly want to be in Europe and allow that little bit of sea called the English Channel to be the moat around the castle they call home. What the American visitor might call misanthropy could equally be called 'a desire for privacy'. The continentals are for ever in the street chatting and flirting but it is the English who polish their bikes in the confines of their back garden and given that the English dream might be for privacy without loneliness, the obvious solution to this peculiar problem is to own a house.

Communal space such as flats or housing association projects sit poorly on the shoulders of the English householder. In France, Italy and Germany it is estimated that half of all new-builds are flats and apartments, compared to about 15% here. Once a bloke has come in from his bike ride, he wants to shut his own front door. A study of British political life done at the turn of the century by the German writer and architect, Hermann Muthesius centred on the concept of *'Das Englische Haus'*. Perhaps a bit boring if you are not an architect or town planner but it extended into three volumes and helped to make his reputation. Muthesius concluded that *'there is nothing as unique in English architecture as the development of the house'*. He also commented about the *'tasteless speculative housing, with whole acres covered with wretched, absolutely uniform small houses'*.

To really and truly understand what it means to ride your bike in England, around the coast of Britain, from the café and back, must be to understand a little of your environment – to push the envelope a little further than 'because it's there'. When climbers scale Everest and claim to do it simply 'because it's there' I find this rather patronising as an explanation. I know it's there, what I want to know is *why* people climb it or swim across a windy sea? All summer I have ridden, in and around large towns and cities, between Great Yarmouth and Southend, Portsmouth to Plymouth and much more besides. Whole suburbs full of trivial façades have been designed without understanding and in a nuclear style of living reduced to its smallest parts, thousands upon thousands of identikit houses that testify to the Englishman's love of his home as his castle and a questionable independence of mind. At Berwick I am fed into the one-way system until I park on the main street outside a Caffé Nero for a hot drink. While the city is known for its walls and decades of bloody history, I see only the aesthetic compromise forced on us by town planners, unimaginative developers and chain-store management. Holland & Barrett is next to New Look and Boots is adjacent to Superdrug. Shop names like Burton, Phones4U and Clinton the card shop are places of commercial activity replicated exactly through towns and cities across Britain. In the face of such a miasma of corporate mediocrity, is it any wonder you look to the past to get a clue as to what the future might hold?

Along with religion and property, perhaps as much as anything which influences how we think, it is the weather that rubs and washes our soul. Between Alnwick and Ashington and then onto Newcastle and Gateshead the rain is falling heavily.

Anglo-Saxon poetry tells of a land, frozen with cold icicles; how the water's torrent shrank in the rivers and *'ice-bridged the dark ocean road'*. It is a silent and empty England, the Saxon Kingdom. Chieftains and kings of the period in damp chambers in their castles would have known of the coldness that blew along their corridors.

King Alfred himself would have blustered against the wind that pierced cracks in the corners where candles were blown out by sudden draughts. The haunting image of a solitary sparrow, flying into a warm banqueting hall, from a dark night laden with deeply penetrating rain, is all the more poignant when you see her fly out again. For a moment warm and languid in a space sweetened by the cushion of cooked meats and mead only to vanish into a wintry world and not to be seen again. It is as if winter discloses the true nature of the English imagination. Charlotte Brontë wrote in Jane Eyre of *'a ceaseless rain sweeping away wildly before a long and lamentable blast'*. Like all of us on such a day, Jane herself dreams of warm desolate shores and standing alone amidst a sea of billow and spray. In such a poem there was always loud and moaning winds and windows shaking with fitful bursts of weather and always the impenetrable black night.

In a sense, as I ride down the east coast of England, back to the beginning of the journey, I now realise that whatever it was this trip purported to be at the start, it is not the same at the finish. In one sense I thank anyone's God for that. Rhetorical outbursts of a desperate need to understand may only have highlighted further confusion, but what is a journey if it isn't there to entertain and to inform, to propel you somewhere from your comfortable eyrie. If I were to climb Everest it would not just be to stand on the top but also to know what the top is made of. In my experience, riding a motorcycle around the world is nearly impossibly hard to start, but it's very sweet to finish.

As I ride between Whitby and Scarborough to drink my coke in the Barracuda Bar it is what I can now call my final bit. I have Bridlington and Hull yet to do and a last gasp to North Norfolk to complete the circle, but there is also a point in a journey – an adventure that has taken thirty years – whereby you do not need to move any more. The bike can stay in the shed and the mind can do the travelling. As a world biker I would say that the fulfilment of a dream has an obviousness about it, and it is partly down to the ability to be able to dream. The better you can dream, the less need you have to go and it is this point where my journeying is beginning to take me.

Review of Parallel World

I've long been baffled by Nick Sanders' approach to world travel. The first time I saw a picture of him in racing leathers and full face helmet I asked myself what on earth he was up to. *'That's no way to travel the world on a motorcycle.'* I said, *'you'll absorb nothing rushing about with a goldfish bowl on your head and dressed for racing.'*

This latest book calls a lie to my fondly nurtured prejudices. Like all lazy reviewers I'll fill a paragraph with a quote.

"As a traveller you become psychologist, counsellor, futurologist, judge, diplomat and clown. It is the responsibility of the traveller to look sincere and caring at all times. You take a hippocratic oath not to patronise or condescend or be too obsequious whilst the most miserable looking lag weighs you down with yet more heinous tittle tattle and leave feeling a little lighter."

Pithy comment like this litters a book that breaks new ground in my limited reading experience as a pictorial diary par excellence.

The overview of nations, landscapes and cultures is balanced by the micro study of a beetle crossing a coffee stained table at which Sanders is seated between bouts of missile man velocity. It's good to see that even an R1 in Nick's obviously capable hands is reduced to bicycle speeds by mud and sand however. At one point the supreme sports bike is coaxed along at 9mph for 15 hour days through what looks like a ploughed field several hundred miles across. I was relieved to see that some of these pictures show the rider in shirt sleeves and cargo pants rather than ubiquitous one piece leathers.

Written during his 35,000 mile Parallel World tour through 41 countries Nick somehow found enough time, after riding for 12 hours each day on average, to pen the text of this superb book. He is also responsible for the gallery of fabulous atmospheric pictures which he has somehow found the time to record. These are not mere snapshots grabbed from the saddle with a compact as the engine ticks over. These are thoughtful high quality arty images including many people portraits that capture the spirit of the lands through which he has passed, sometimes at ludicrous speed.

How does he do it? I am reminded of a phrase levelled by a Glaswegian opponent of an old friend of mine who used to enter eating contests for money. *'The man is noo natural!'*

The format of the fat 288 page book is a little unusual being about 10 inches square but it works well. The text overlays parts of some pictures that have been faded to ghost strength so there is no problem reading. The large majority of pictures are stand alone paintings of quite astonishing vibrancy. It is the perfect pick it up, read a section and come back to it book with a very modest cover price of £12.95. It can be bought with the two DVDs for £30. A blinding deal but I still can't see how he can wear a full face helmet in hot countries. The man is noo natural.

Ian Mutch

First published in 2009 by Nick Sanders Books
Machynlleth, Wales
www.nicksanders.com
© Photographs 2009 Nick Sanders
Chippy Wood and Joshua Wyborn
© Text 2009 Nick Sanders

ISBN: 978-0-9549081-8-8
This book is sold subject to the condition that it may not be resold or otherwise issued except in its original binding.

A CIP catalogue record for this book is available from the British Library. British Library Cataloguing-in-Publication Data.

Repro, printing and binding: Singapore, under the supervision of MRM Graphics, Winslow, Buckinghamshire.